AF432135

9 789991 699186

Ranald MacDonald

A Manga of His Adventure in Japan

By Akiko Shimojima
and Sean Michael Wilson

EOSTRE

First published in 2024 by Eostre Publications
of Tallinn, Estonia.

Book design by Ian Sharman

Edited by Sean Michael Wilson and Koit Rikson

Printed in 2024

ISBN: 978-9916-9918-6-2

From the Fog of History, a New Hero Emerges

I have always believed the mid-19th century adventurer, Ranald MacDonald, should be far better known than he is. He risked his life in 1848 to enter Japan when it was "closed" to the outside world — when, after over two hundred years, the Tokugawa Shogunate still prohibited Japanese from leaving and banned foreigners (save for a few Dutch and Chinese traders in Nagasaki) from entering. Punishments could even include execution. If that were not enough of a deterrent, in 1848 there was also no simple way for someone like Ranald — unconnected to any organization or government — to even get to Japan. Today, it would be like an individual deciding to go to the Moon on their own, and somehow doing so.

Ranald was born near the mouth of the Columbia River in 1824, in what is now known as Astoria, Oregon, by the Pacific Ocean. The "United States" was then twenty-four far-away states, all east of the Rocky Mountains. "Oregon" was a vast area between the Rockies and the Pacific, covering today's Oregon and Washington states, as well as Canada's British Columbia — a largely unexplored wilderness inhabited by a multitude of Native American tribes and claimed by Britain, the United States, and Russia. The few Europeans in the area were fur traders, and all men. There were no white women west of the Rockies.

Ranald's mother was Koale'xoa, daughter of Comcomly, the famous chief of the Chinook tribe who met the Lewis and Clarke Expedition to the Pacific Ocean in 1805. Ranald's father, Archibald McDonald, of Scottish descent, was an officer in the Hudson's Bay Company — a powerful fur trading organization that functioned like an independent corporate state. Licensed by the British Crown, it had the power to deploy its own armies and navies, make laws, and mint coin, and it operated over a vast area named Rupert's Land in central Canada, extending south into today's Minnesota. In the early years, employees were encouraged to marry native women, which resulted in a unique culture around trading posts. As a child, Ranald was first schooled in the multi-racial, polyglot culture of Fort Vancouver, upstream from Astoria on the Columbia. When ten, he was sent across the Rockies to Red River, in today's Winnipeg, Canada, where mixed-race children of Company officers could receive a more advanced education. Always intelligent, it is here that Ranald became highly literate for his time. Red River was a unique environment, and long after he left, in 1869–70, it became the site of the last independent nation declared in North America, during a rebellion by *Metis* or mixed-race fur-trade descendants.

Ranald's life and adventure to Japan provide us a view of history that transcends normal national narratives. For an ordinary individual, he is surprisingly well-documented, but his background and life were so exotic that many mysteries, myths, and misunderstandings persist. Contrary to what some have written, Ranald just missed meeting three Japanese castaways who wound up in Fort Vancouver in 1834; there is no evidence that he taught them English or learned Japanese then. There is no doubt, however, that he knew of them and that someone, at some point, told him that he resembled Japanese people. Yet his true goal in entering Japan is still veiled in mystery. Did he want to use his linguistic skills to become an interpreter, or a trader like his father? And why did he take a copy of the Bible? Sailors in his era knew this could result in execution (as Christianity was outlawed in Japan), so what was he thinking? We may never know exactly.

Such mysteries aside, Ranald's sojourn in Japan can nonetheless be corroborated directly from a remarkable number of sources — from his own accounts; from surviving Japanese interrogation records; from mentions in the journal of a Dutch trader in Nagasaki; from an 1849 deposition taken aboard the U.S. Navy ship, "*Preble*", that retrieved him from Nagasaki; from an interview conducted by a British official on disembarking in Hong Kong; and from a rare, surviving 1849 letter he sent from Hong Kong to an American missionary in Hawaii.

Japanese records of his interrogations in Nagasaki are surprisingly accurate. In those days, no Japanese interpreters knew English (only Dutch and Chinese), so a Dutch trader first translated Ranald's English responses into Dutch. The Japanese interpreters then translated the Dutch into Japanese for the local magistrate. Despite this, Ranald's deposition shows him telling his captors that he is from places then unknown to them, such as *Kanada* (Canada), *Oregon* (19th century "Oregon"), *Roburutsurando* (Rupert's Land), *Sagu Haruhoru* (Sag Harbor, New York), and even giving them the names of his ship, *Purimouto* ("*Plymouth*") and his captain, *Etowaru* (Lawrence B. Edwards).

When Ranald's adventure to Japan was widely reported in the United States in 1849 and 1850, he was already off to new adventures in other lands, where he largely disappears from the historical record. When he returned to North America in 1853, public fascination with Japan had begun to shift, and was soon dominated by news of attempts by Commodore Matthew Perry and the U.S. Navy to force Japan to open to the outside world. References to Ranald thereafter appear occasionally in local papers in the Pacific Northwest of both Canada and the United States, but his next, most prominently documented adventure was as a member of Robert Brown's famous 1864 Vancouver Island Exploring

Expedition. Near the end of his life, corresponding with Malcolm McLeod—a mixed-race family friend and lawyer in Ottawa, who served as his editor—he finally began to work seriously on a narrative of his life and his Japan adventure. It was never published while he was alive. In 1891, three years before he died, he gained considerable publicity when he was interviewed at old Fort Colvile, in Washington, by journalist Elizabeth B. Custer for the *Harper's Weekly*, a popular American publication of the time. He tried to describe his life and his adventure to Japan to her, but her condescending article deeply angered him. She was the widow of George A. Custer, the famous general who had died fifteen years earlier fighting Native Americans at the Battle of the Little Big Horn. While charmed by his personality and exoticism, she was unable to set aside her racial prejudices. And in trying to convey his Japan adventure she mistakenly placed him in China.

In recent decades more people have become interested in Ranald. "Friends of MacDonald" societies have sprouted in Japan, the United States, Canada, and the Netherlands. In English, an annotated and heavily edited, posthumously published 1923 version of his "autobiography," was published in 1923 and there are biographies from 1906, 1940, 1997, 2003, and 2008. There is a monument to his birthplace in Astoria, Oregon. His gravesite, in far northeastern Washington near the border with Canada, is now the state's tiniest state park, with historical markers. Although half Chinook, Ranald died a member of the Lake tribe, part of the Colville Federated Tribes nearby, at what was then the ripe old age of seventy.

In Japan, where Ranald is best known, he has appeared in academic and popular books, and in documentaries and dramas. There are monuments to him in the far north, on Rishiri Island, where he landed, and in the city of Nagasaki, where he was imprisoned. A vocabulary list of Japanese words that he secretly compiled survives in British Columbia and has also been heavily studied by Japanese linguists; it demonstrates his own language skills.

When Ranald is described in Japan, it is usually as "the first teacher of English," even though this technically is probably not true. What really matters most is to *whom* Ranald taught English, and *when*, for his pupils included prominent professional government interpreters (who then only knew Dutch). This helped Japan greatly later when it came time to delicately negotiate the country's opening with demanding foreign—especially American and British—officials. In 2024, on the 100th anniversary of Ranald's birth, Japan Post issued an official ¥84 stamp which proclaims him to be the "First English Teacher in Japan."

With this pioneering manga—a graphic novel that is not a novel but a visual documentary—we have a wonderful and brand-new take on the story of Ranald MacDonald. And it will surely interest ever-more people in his amazing and heroic adventure. Kudos to Sean Michael Wilson, the writer, and Akiko Shimojima, the artist, and the people at Eostre Publications, for their hard work!

Frederik L. Schodt is an award-winning writer and translator in the San Francisco Bay Area. He is the author of *Native American in the Land of the Shogun: Ranald MacDonald and the Opening of Japan*. (Berkeley: Stone Bridge Press, 2003). In 2009 he received the Order of the Rising Sun, Gold Rays with Rosette, for helping to popularize Japanese popular culture in North America.

THIS IS THE STORY OF WHY AND HOW RANALD MACDONALD ENTERED JAPAN IN 1848, ON HIS OWN, DESPITE THE RULES FORBIDDING SUCH A STRANGE ADVENTURE.

1

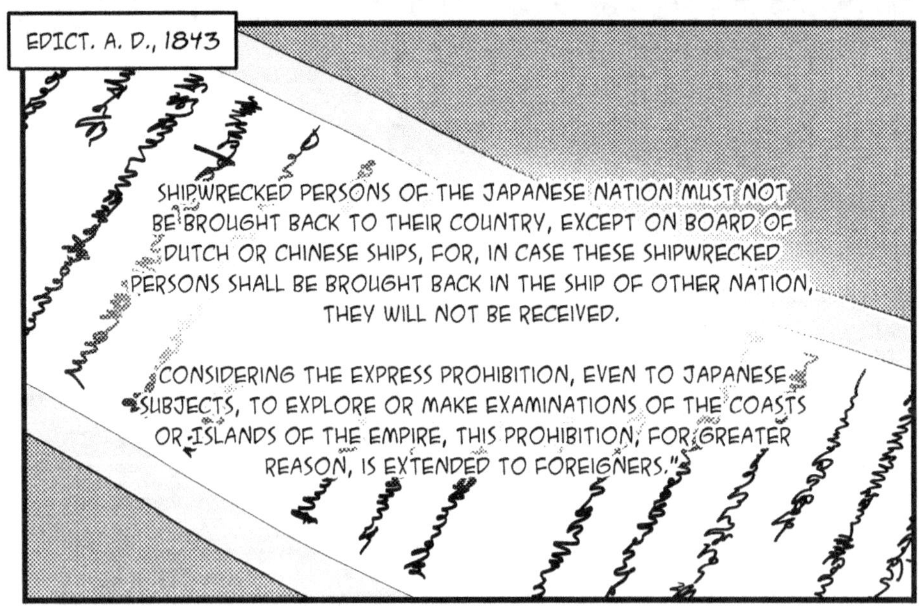

* MACDONALD'S MEMOIRS INCORRECTLY NOTES THIS AS FROM 1837, BUT THE MAIN ANNOUNCEMENT FROM THE TOKUGAWA GOVERNMENT WAS 'THE EDICT OF 1635 ORDERING THE CLOSING OF JAPAN'. IN TOTAL 5 SUCH DOCUMENTS WERE ISSUED BETWEEN 1633 AND 1639. THE LOWER EDICT SEEMS TO HAVE BEEN GIVEN TO THE DUTCH AND DISTRIBUTED BY THEM TO OTHER NATIONALITIES. MACDONALD SEEMS TO HAVE GOTTEN THIS FROM RICHARD HILDRETH'S 1855 BOOK 'JAPAN. AS IT WAS, AND IS', WHO TOOK SOME INFORMATION FROM DR. ENGELBERT KAEMPFER'S POSTHUMOUSLY PUBLISHED 1727 BOOK 'HISTORY OF JAPAN'.

UTOPIA OF THE HOARY EAST! TO US, ON ITS OPPOSITE SHORE, GAZING SEARCHINGLY INTO THE FAR DISTANCE IT WAS EVER AN OBJECT OF INTENSE CURIOSITY. WHAT OF SUCH PEOPLE?

SUCH WAS THE WALL OF FIRE AROUND THEIR OWN BELOVED ISLES, OF THE JAPANESE PEOPLE, EMINENTLY A WARRIOR RACE, WHO HAD REPELLED ALL POWERS—FROM KUBLAI KHAN TO THE PRESENT—FROM HOSTILE TOUCH.

DEEPLY MOVED, I RESOLVED TO PERSONALLY SOLVE THE MYSTERY, IF POSSIBLE, AT ANY COST OF EFFORT — EVEN TO LIFE ITSELF. THE PRESENT IS THE STORY OF IT...

THESE QUESTIONS WERE OFTEN THE TALK AMONGST THE ELDERS OF THE CHINOOK PEOPLE OF COLUMBIA AREA. THIS WAS MY MOTHER'S TRIBE, HER FATHER BEING KING COM-COMLY.

MY PLAN WAS TO DISGUISE MY MOTIVE AND PRESENT MYSELF AS A CASTAWAY; AND TO RELY ON THEIR HUMANITY. I COULD NOT BELIEVE THEM WHOLLY LOST TO IT.

SATISFIED IN MY OWN CONSCIENCE WITH THIS PURPOSE, I NEVER ABANDONED IT. THAT PURPOSE WAS TO LEARN OF THEM; AND, IF POSSIBLE, TO INSTRUCT THEM OF US.

I TOOK A SMALL COLLECTION OF BOOKS WITH ME: A SIMPLE ENGLISH BIBLE, PRAYER BOOK (CHURCH OF ENGLAND), A DICTIONARY, GRAMMAR, HISTORY, AND GEOGRAPHY.
I WAS NOT A GREAT MAN OF LEARNING, BUT ALWAYS A LOVER OF BOOKS.

"HAVE FAITH IN ONE ANOTHER" IS A MOTTO I HAVE CHERISHED. IT REQUIRES CAUTION, AND THERE IS EVER AN ELEMENT OF RISK IN IT: BUT THAT IS THE SPICE OF LIFE.

BEING A PEOPLE OF LITERATURE AND BOOKS, I THOUGHT THESE MIGHT BE WELL RECEIVED. IN FACT IT WAS THAT WHICH SAVED ME:
FOR SEEING ME EVER READING, THEY DREW TO ME: THE BOOKS MAGNETIZED THEM, AND THEY MADE ME THEIR TEACHER!
FOR MEANS TO CARRY IT OUT, I SIMPLY, WITH GRIP SACK IN HAND, WALKED FORTH INTO THE DARKNESS OF AN UNSYMPATHETIC WORLD;
ALONE, TELLING NO ONE; WITH BARELY SCRIPT FOR THE HOUR.
THAT WAS IN 1845, WHEN I WAS JUST TWENTY ONE; IN THE FREEDOM OF MANHOOD; WITH FULL VIGOUR OF YOUTH. I WENT WEST TO THE MISSISSIPPI AND GOT WORK AS A BOAT HAND ON ONE OF ITS PALACE STEAMERS.

*AT THAT TIME, THE SANDWICH ISLANDS WAS THE NAME FOR THE HAWAIIAN ISLANDS.

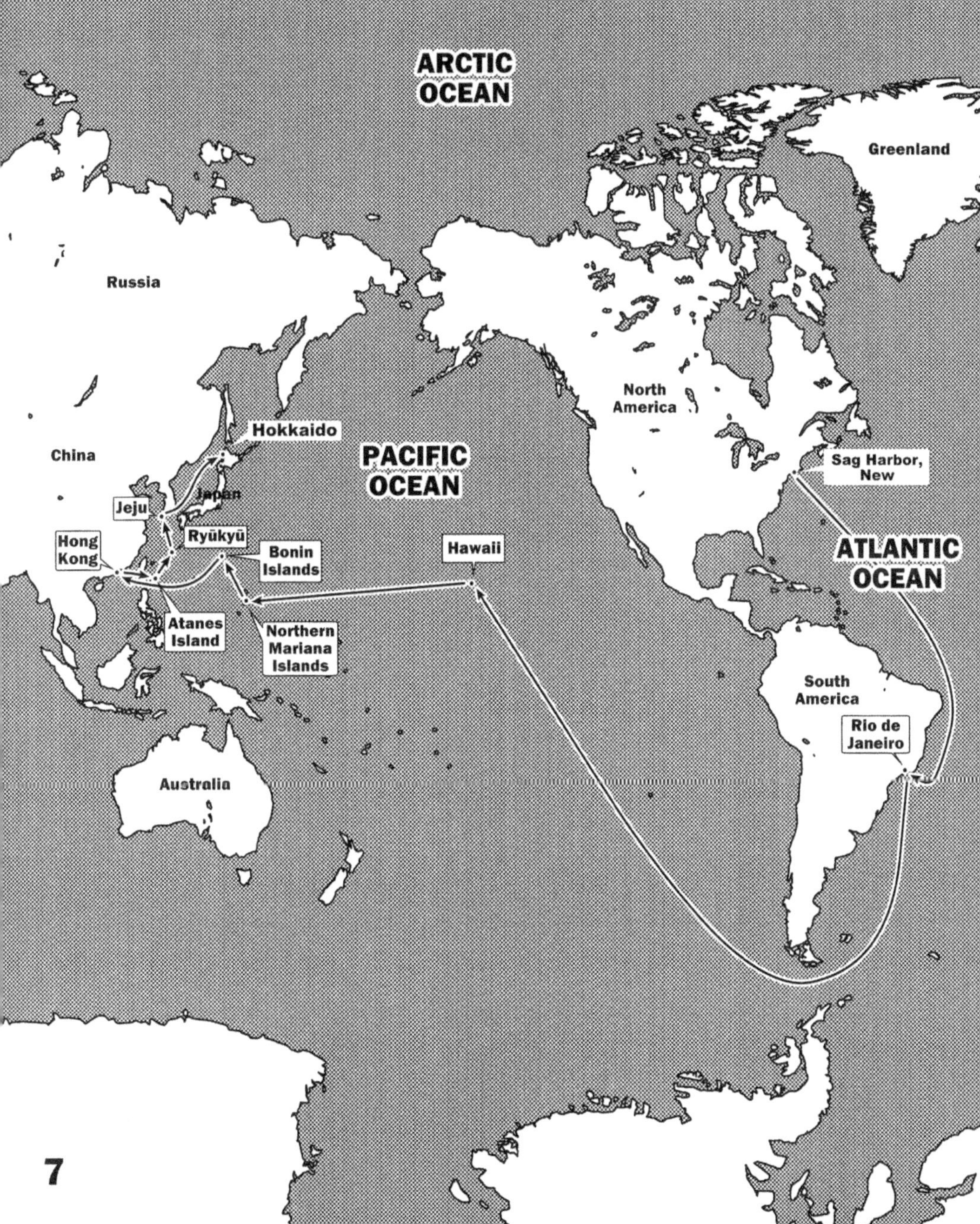

THE ROUTE FROM NEW YORK TO HOKKAIDO.
ARCTIC OCEAN
Greenland
Russia
North America
China
Hokkaido
PACIFIC OCEAN
Japan
Jeju
Ryūkyū
Hong Kong
Bonin Islands
Hawaii
Sag Harbor, New
ATLANTIC OCEAN
Atanes Island
Northern Mariana Islands
South America
Rio de Janeiro
Australia

*1 RANALD MACDONALD MAY HAVE ARRANGED THIS IN LAHAINA IN HAWAII IN LATE 1846 OR EARLY 1847.

*2 THE "PLYMOUTH" AND THE "DAVID PADDOCK" SPENT A YEAR AND A HALF IN HAWAII, SOMETIMES GOING ON WHALING EXPEDITIONS, UNTIL LEAVING IN NOVEMBER 1847. BUT, ODDILY, RANALD MACDONALD DOES NOT MENTION THIS IN HIS MEMOIR.

*1 THE LADRONES ISLANDS ARE COMMONLY KNOWN TODAY AS THE MARIANA ISLANDS.

*2 ISLAND OF GREGAN IS NOW AGRIHAN IN THE NORTHERN MARIANAS.

9

IT'S BEEN MANY A YEAR SINCE WE HAD VISITORS LIKE YOURSELVES.
WELL MET FELLOWS! I'M LIVERPOOL JACK, I AM.

BUT WE ARE NOT ON BEST TERMS.
I CLAIM A CERTAIN CHILD IS MINE. HE CLAIMS IT IS HIS.

THERE IS ANOTHER WHITE MAN, LIVING ABOUT A MILE NORTH, "SPIDER JACK", WHO LIVES WITH A SICKLY WIFE.
I HAVE BEEN HERE FOURTEEN OR FIFTEEN YEARS NOW. SPIDER JACK ABOUT FOUR YEARS LONGER THAN THAT.

SPIDER JOINED US LATER AND THEY PUT ASIDE THEIR DISAGREEMENT FOR THE TIME BEING TO EXPLAIN VARIOUS THINGS TO US.

THEIR WEALTH CONSISTED OF PIGS AND CHICKENS: THE MORE WIVES THEY HAD, THE MORE PIGS AND CHICKENS THEY COULD ATTEND TO.

ONCE THERE HAD BEEN ABOUT 20 OF THEM, BUT THERE HAD BEEN SEVERAL FIGHTS; AND MURDERS HAD TAKEN PLACE AMONG THEM.

WE LEARNED THAT HAVING BEEN LOST AT SEA IN A LARGE CANOE THEY WERE FOUND BY A PASSING SHIP. THE CAPTAIN LATER DEPOSITED THEM ON GREGAN GIVING THEM A SOW WITH A PIG, A COCK, AND A COUPLE OF HENS, WHICH HAD GREATLY MULTIPLIED SINCE THEN.
THERE BE A LARGE AMOUNT OF TREASURE BURIED IN THE ISLAND OF PEGAN, NEAR HERE: WE KNOW THE EXACT SPOT.

TO CORROBORATE THIS, ONE OF OUR MEN WHO HAD TIME TO ACCEPT SPIDER JACK'S INVITATION TO VISIT HIS HUT OR HOUSE REPORTED SEEING THERE HALF A CHESTFUL OF SILVER DOLLARS: AND THAT JACK TRIED TO PERSUADE HIM TO DESERT THE SHIP. HE DECLINED; FROM FEAR OF BEING MURDERED.

WISELY IGNORING THE FANTASY OF THE POSSIBLE TREASURE WE STEERED WEST, KEEPING A LITTLE NORTH SO AS TO SIGHT THE BONIN ISLANDS, THINKING WE MIGHT FIND SPERM WHALES.

FROM THERE WE WENT TO THE BASHEE ISLANDS *1, SPANISH POSSESSIONS, SOUTH OF THE ISLAND OF FORMOSA *2. THERE WE LANDED ON BATAN ISLAND, WHICH POSSESSED A GOOD THOUGH SMALL HARBOR.

ITS CAPITAL CONSISTED OF VERY MISERABLE HUTS, BUT THE "GOVERNOR'S PALACE" AND A PLACE OF WORSHIP WERE BUILT OF STONE.
HERE WE GOT SOME YAMS, A FEW ONIONS, AND SOME BEEF.
*1 BASHEE ISLANDS ARE NOW BATANES ISLANDS.
*2 FORMASA IS NOW TAIWAN.

AFTER WE LEFT THE BASHEES, WE FELL IN WITH THE FIRST SCHOOL OF WHALES— SPERM WHALES—AND KILLED A GREAT MANY.

WE THENCE STEERED FOR HONG KONG, WHERE WE STRIPT, AND LAID OVER FOR A MONTH, FITTING OUT FOR A CRUISE IN THE JAPAN SEA.

ON OUR FIRST VISIT THERE, WE GAVE THE NATIVES POTATOES FOR SEED: THEY HAD NOT HAD ANY FOR SOME YEARS. WE ALSO FURNISHED THEM WITH SOME BEANS AND INDIAN CORN, THOUGH THEY HAD PLENTY OF EACH, BUT OUR GRAIN WAS LARGER THAN THEIRS AND THEY PREFERRED IT.

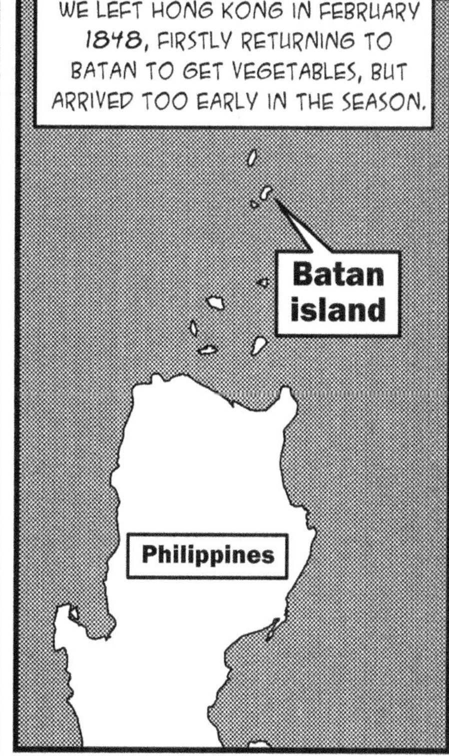

WE LEFT HONG KONG IN FEBRUARY 1848, FIRSTLY RETURNING TO BATAN TO GET VEGETABLES, BUT ARRIVED TOO EARLY IN THE SEASON.

Batan island
Philippines

15

* LOO-CHOO ISLANDS = THE RYUKYU ISLANDS. QUELPERT ISLAND = CHEJU ISLAND OR JEJU ISLAND, NOW PART OF SOUTH KOREA.

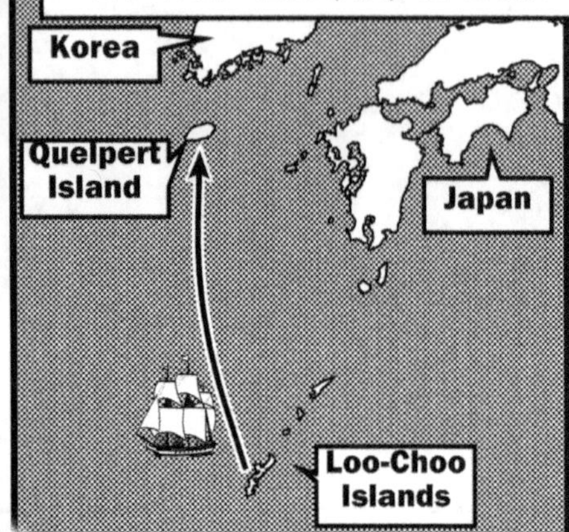

LEAVING THE BASHEES WE SAILED BY THE LOO-CHOO ISLANDS TO THE TONGHAI SEA, AND THEN TO QUELPERT ISLAND.* A BEAUTIFUL ISLAND SITUATED NEAR THE STRAITS OF KOREA, ABOUT 120 MILES FROM NAGASAKI IN JAPAN, AND WITHIN ABOUT 250 MILES FROM THE MOUTHS OF THE HOANGHO AND YANG-TZSE RIVERS OF CHINA.
Korea
Quelpert Island
Japan
Loo-Choo Islands
CHINA IS A LAND OF UPWARDS OF THREE HUNDRED MILLION INDUSTRIOUS PEOPLE. THE CRADLE, HOME, AND CEMETERY OF NEARLY ONE FOURTH OF OUR FELLOWMEN ON EARTH.
A PEOPLE OF A HIGH CIVILIZATION; WITH MORAL, INTELLECTUAL, AND PHYSICAL APTITUDES REQUIRING BUT THE SYMPATHETIC TOUCH OF OUR MORE UTILITARIAN DYNAMICS OF LIFE TO WIN THEM TO A CLOSER COMITY IN THE FAMILY OF NATIONS.

ON THIS THEME, MY IDEAS MAY SEEM WILD, BUT THEY ARE THE CONCLUSIONS OF PERSONAL OBSERVATION. WHAT THE FUTURE, UNDER THE PROVIDENCE OF THE GREAT FATHER OF ALL, MAY HAVE IN STORE FOR US I LEAVE TO THE LOGIC OF EVENTS TO DEVELOP.

FORTIFIED, AND HELD BY A NAVAL POWER IT MIGHT BE MADE THE MALTA OF THE EAST, AND EVEN OF THE VASTER NORTHERN PACIFIC. RUSSIA MAY TAKE IT, SINCE THAT RISING POWER'S VLADIVOSTOK (ICE BOUND IN WINTER) DOES NOT SECURE HER ANCHORAGE IN THE JUNK THRONGED SEAS OF CHINA AND JAPAN.

WE FISHED ABOUT THE QUELPERT ISLAND FOR ABOUT A WEEK. ITS TEMPERATURE IS COOLER AND HEALTHIER THAN HONG KONG, WITH ABUNDANT VEGETATION AND WITH EVERY RESOURCE AND FACILITY FOR SHIP SUPPLIES.

AT LENGTH WE LEFT IT, AND ON MARCH 6TH ENTERED THE JAPAN SEA PROPER. FOR ABOUT THREE MONTHS WE HAD CALMS OR VERY LIGHT BREEZES, SCARCELY ENOUGH TO FILL OUR TOP SAILS. THOUGH OFTEN A GOOD DEAL OF FOG, ESPECIALLY WHILE IN THE CHANNEL OF TARTARY.

WHALING WAS SO EASY IN THE JAPAN SEA - THE FISH WERE SO NUMEROUS THAT WE HAD NO OCCASION TO CHASE THEM WITH OUR SHIP. WE HAD ONLY TO LOWER OUR BOATS, HARPOON THEM, AND BRING THEM ALONGSIDE FOR STRIPPING. IN THE FOREPART OF THE SEASON WE TOOK SEVERAL WHALES.

NOW AND HERE WOULD BE A GOOD PLACE TO LET ME TAKE MY LEAVE, DEAR CAPTAIN.
NO, NO, COME ON NOW MAN. LET'S HEAR NO MORE OF THIS FOOLISHNESS.
AT LENGTH ON JUNE 27TH, 1848, THE SHIP BEING THEN FULL AND LYING OFF THE COAST OF JAPAN, ABOUT FIVE MILES FROM THE NEAREST ISLAND, I ASKED THE CAPTAIN TO LET ME LEAVE THE SHIP.
I MUST PRESS YOU TO REMEMBER OUR BARGAIN, MY CAPTAIN.
BARGAIN, WHAT BARGAIN? I REMEMBER NOTHING.
AH, YOU ARE A KIND GENTLEMAN INDEED TO PRETEND LIKE THIS. BUT I MUST INSIST. I SHALL HAVE MY ADVENTURE.
OH, YOU MAD FOOL!
19

* $600 IN 1848 IS MORE THAN $23,000 TODAY.

A SAILOR'S FEELINGS ARE EVER WARM AND TRUE. THE COMPANIONSHIP OF PERIL FORGES A MASONIC BOND STRONGER THAN MERE WORLDLY INTEREST.

MY COMRADES REFUSED TO UNLOOSE THE KNOT WHICH BOUND ME TO THEM.
CAST ME OFF NOW, MY DEAR COMRADES.
NO, WE WON'T!

WITH AVERTED FACE, HAD TO CUT THE ROPE MYSELF. I FELT IN THE CORD A STRONG ELECTRIC SYMPATHY BURSTING FROM THE TRUE FRIENDLY HEARTS OF MY COMRADES.

"HAPPY TO MEET; SORRY TO PART", IS EVER TRUTH WITH HIM. A SAILOR, EVEN IN HIS MANHOOD, HAS TEARS!
WE'LL NEVER SEE YOU AGAIN DEAR MAC!

GOD BLESS YOU MAC!
THEY BADE ME A LONG, AND, AS THEY THOUGHT, A LAST ADIEU! IT WAS INDEED SO, FOR I HAVE SEEN NONE OF THEM SINCE, SAVE ONE, THE CAPTAIN.

SO, WE PARTED. THEY "HOMEWARD BOUND!" I, FOR THE MYSTERIOUS JAPAN! BUT MY MIND WAS FIXED; AND MY HOT HEART, FULL OF ITS PURPOSE, SWELLED IN UNISON WITH THE PACIFIC BILLOW.

SHE HOISTED AND DIPPED HER STARS AND STRIPES FLAG TO ME SEVERAL TIMES, WHICH I ANSWERED BY DIPPING A LITTLE WHITE FLAG WHICH I HAD.

22

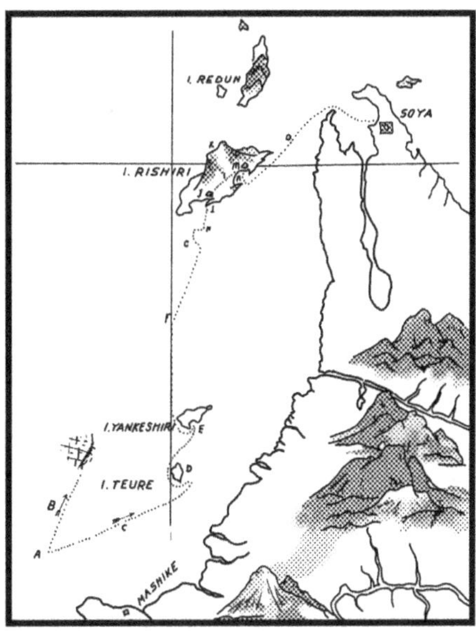

*1 TODAY CALLED TEURI ISLAND
*2 TODAY CALLED YAGISHIRI ISLAND

HERE I FELL IN WITH A HERD OF SEA LIONS, MAKING A GREAT NOISE, A COMPOUND OF THE BARK OF A LARGE DEEP-MOUTHED DOG AND THE BELLOW OF A BULL.
WO!
WO!

I SUCCEEDED IN GETTING TO THE LEEWARD OF THE ISLAND BY WEARING ROUND MY BOAT AND SETTING THE AFT SAIL ALL SQUARE.

WO!

THESE ANIMALS WERE ABOUT TWELVE FEET IN LENGTH; WEIGHING PROBABLY ABOUT TEN OR TWELVE HUNDREDWEIGHT. TO TEST MY PISTOL I SHOT ONE.

*ACTUALLY YAGISHIRI ISLAND WAS INHABITED THEN, BUT MACDONALD DID NOT EXPLORE THE OTHER SIDE OF THE ISLAND, WHERE A SMALL FISHING OUTPOST WAS ESTABLISHED IN 1746.

SO FAR AS I COULD SEE, IT WAS CONTESTED ONLY BY INNUMERABLE DUCKS, GEESE AND OTHER WATER FOWL.
NEXT MORNING I AWOKE REFRESHED, AND AFTER A BREAKFAST ON BEEF, BISCUIT AND CHOCOLATE, I STARTED ON AN EXPLORATION OF MY NEW DOMINION.
ON IT I SPENT A ROBINSON CRUSOE LIFE FOR TWO DAYS, (28TH AND 29TH JUNE); MATURING, DURING THAT TIME, MY PLAN OF INVASION.
I FOUND THE ISLAND COVERED WITH SMALL TREES AND BUSHES (OF NAMES UNKNOWN TO ME), CANE BRAKE, AND SWARD, THE WHOLE PICTURESQUELY DOTTED WITH LAKELETS AND PONDS.

* RISHIRI ISLAND, THIS IS ALSO MENTIONED IN OUR BOOK, MAMIYA'S MAPS, PUBLISHED BY EOSTRE IN *2022*, AS ONE OF THE PLACES THAT RUSSIAN FORCES ATTACKED IN *1807*, 41 YEARS BEFORE MACDONALD LANDED THERE.

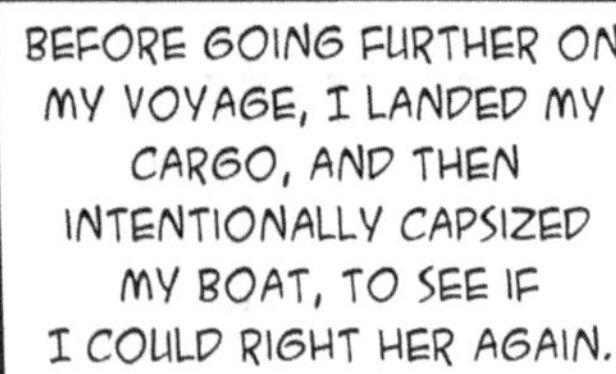

BEFORE GOING FURTHER ON MY VOYAGE, I LANDED MY CARGO, AND THEN INTENTIONALLY CAPSIZED MY BOAT, TO SEE IF I COULD RIGHT HER AGAIN.

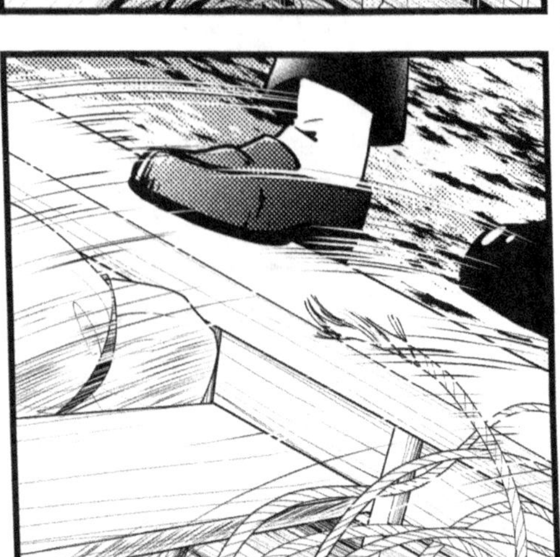

MY DESIGN IN THIS WAS TO PRESENT MYSELF IN DISTRESS; FOR, WITH ALL THEIR REPUTED CRUELTY TO FOREIGNERS, I HALF BELIEVED THAT THE JAPANESE WOULD HAVE SOME COMPASSION TOWARDS THOSE THAT STORM OR UNCONTROLLABLE CIRCUMSTANCES CAST UPON THEIR SHORES.

MY CHEST AND AN OAR I RECOVERED WITH SOME DIFFICULTY— THE OAR FOR STEERING AS I HAD TO LET THE RUDDER GO. SATISFIED WITH THE RESULT, I RETURNED AND SPENT ANOTHER NIGHT ON MY ISLAND.

AFTER SUCCESSFULLY DOING THAT A POTENTIAL DISASTROUS THING HAPPENED.

NEXT MORNING (JULY 1ST), I STARTED FOR THE LARGE ISLAND. SUPPOSING THE ISLAND TO BE INHABITED, I DESIGNEDLY UPSET MY BOAT AGAIN ABOUT FIVE OR SIX MILES TO THE LEEWARD OF IT.

WiiiSHH!

SPLLAASH!

I CAPTURED MY CHEST FIRST, BUT UNFORTUNATELY IT WAS UNLOCKED AND MANY THINGS FELL OUT.

MY BREAD BISCUITS AND MY COMPASS WAS GONE.

BUT THE QUADRANT, BOOKS AND WRITING MATERIALS, ETC., WERE TO THE FORE.

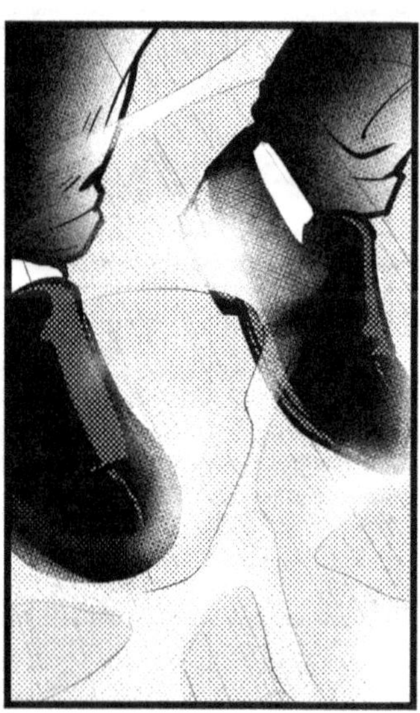

*MACDONALD THOUGHT THEY WERE JAPANESE, BUT ACTUALLY THEY WERE AINU, THE INDIGENOUS PEOPLE OF HOKKAIDO.

AS THEY BOWED THEY UTTERED A GUTTERAL SOUND IN A RESPECTFUL MANNER.

HOW DO YOU DO?
RUWE NE WA!

I FASTENED MY BOAT TO THEIRS, AND JUMPED ON BOARD. THEY DID NOT SEEM TO BE AFRAID OF ME; BUT TO BE WONDER STRUCK AS TO WHO OR WHAT I WAS.

35

I TOOK HOLD OF THE PAIR OF SCULL OARS AND PULLED ABOUT A SHIP'S LENGTH. THEY IMMEDIATELY FOLLOWED MY EXAMPLE, BUT FROM SHEER INABILITY TO KEEP STROKE WITH THEM (THOUGH FAIRLY SMART AT THE OAR) I GAVE UP.

OYAK TA ARPA?
ONE OF THEM, INQUIRINGLY, POINTED TO ONE SIDE OF THE COVE, AND ANOTHER TO THE VILLAGE.

I POINTED TO THE VILLAGE WHICH I HAD SEEN THEM START FROM, SITUATED AT THE FOOT OF A VERY HIGH MOUNTAIN. THE VILLAGE IS A LARGE WOODEN HOUSE SURROUNDED BY A FEW SMALLER HUTS.

36

ON LANDING, I WAS GREETED BY ABOUT A HUNDRED MEN, WOMEN AND CHILDREN—BEING SEATED CROSS-LEGGED ON THE BEACH.

NOT BEING ACCUSTOMED TO THE USE OF SANDALS, I VERY OFTEN STUMBLED.

TWO OF THE BOATSMEN GOT ME A PAIR OF SANDALS FROM ONE OF THE WOMEN, AND PUT THEM ON MY FEET. THEY THEN TOOK ME, GENTLY BY THE WRISTS AND HELPED ME TO ASCEND THE STEEP ROCKY BANK.

I SPOKE SHARPLY TO THEM FOR HURRYING ME OVER THE GROUND. PERCEIVING THAT I WAS DISSATISFIED WITH SOMETHING, THEY RUBBED THEIR PALMS UP AND DOWN AS IF IMPLORING PARDON.

TO AVOID FURTHER HURTING THEIR FEELINGS, I STOOPED TO ADJUST MY SANDALS, BUT THEY INSISTED ON DOING IT THEMSELVES AND APPEARED GLAD TO PERFORM AN ACT OF KINDNESS TO ME.

THINKING THAT HE MIGHT BE A PRIEST I TOUCHED MY HAT TO HIM.
ON APPROACHING THE LARGE HOUSE WE WERE MET BY A MAN WHO LOOKED TO BE A PERSON OF SOME CONSEQUENCE. "
家にあげて やりなさい。
HE REQUESTED ME TO PUT OFF MY SANDALS. I THEN PERCEIVED THAT HE HAD NONE ON. HE THEN LED ME TO A BEDROOM, OFFERING ME A GOWN, AND ADVISING ME TO CHANGE MY CLOTHES— THEN STILL WET—THEN LEFT ME.
"THIS WAS THE FIRST ACTUAL JAPANESE PERSON THAT MACDONALD MET.

AFTER A SHORT INTERVAL, MY HOST INVITED ME TO PARTAKE IN MEAL WHICH HE KINDLY PROVIDED. IT CONSISTED OF BOILED RICE, SOME GOOD FISH (BROILED), GINGER, PRESERVED SHELL FISH, AND A VARIETY OF PICKLES.

ON SMELLING IT—BEING THEN A TEMPERANCE MAN (A TEETOTALLER) I DID NOT TASTE IT—I FOUND IT VERY LIKE WHISKEY. THE LIQUOR IS A DISTILLATION FROM RICE, CALLED SAKI.

BEFORE, AND DURING THE MEAL, MINE HOST SEVERAL TIMES OFFERED ME A BOTTLE OF SOMETHING WHICH HE CALLED:
GROG - YES
NO, THANK YOU.

FETCH IT ON!
GROG? YES!
THE NAME "GROG-YES" PUZZLED ME, ON INQUIRY AFTERWARDS, I LEARNED THAT IT AROSE FROM THE ANSWER OF THE CREW OF THE "LAWRENCE", WHO HAD BEEN IN THAT QUARTER.

I WAS TOLD THAT ONE OF THE MEN OF THE "LAWRENCE" WAS KILLED ATTEMPTING TO ESCAPE WHILE A CAPTIVE WITH THEM. IT DID NOT FRIGHTEN ME.

AFTER BREAKFAST I TOOK A SHORT WALK OUT OF DOORS— THE ONLY FREEDOM I HAD IN JAPAN; AND THAT UNDER CLOSE WATCH.

ON MY RETURN I FOUND THAT MY KIND HOST HAD PROVIDED ME WITH A BED AND A GOOD MOSQUITO BAR. THERE WAS NO BEDSTEAD. I SAW NONE IN THE COUNTRY. NOT HAVING SLEPT THE NIGHT BEFORE, I TURNED IN AND NOW DID SO MOST COMFORTABLY.

40

AT MY REQUEST, MY CLOTHES WERE WASHED IN FRESH WATER, AND DRIED.

IN THE MEANTIME THEY BROUGHT UP MY SAIL, ANCHOR, KEGS, AND CHEST TO THE HOUSE.

YES, STILL WET. I UNDERSTAND.

THANK YOU.

ALL COMMUNICATION SO FAR WAS BY SIGN LANGUAGE.

THEY TOOK A MINUTE INVENTORY OF EVERYTHING BROUGHT ASHORE. EVERYTHING SEEMED TO EXCITE THEIR CURIOSITY—ESPECIALLY MY BOOKS AND LETTERS.

ON THE FOLLOWING DAY, TWO CHIEFS OR OVERSEERS VISITED ME (KETCHINZA AND KEMON, THE FORMER AN AGED MAN).

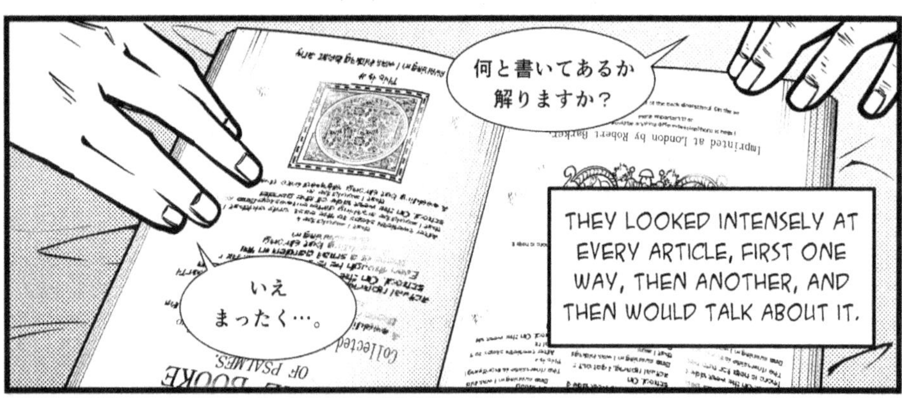

何と書いてあるか
解りますか？
いえ
まったく…。
THEY LOOKED INTENSELY AT EVERY ARTICLE, FIRST ONE WAY, THEN ANOTHER, AND THEN WOULD TALK ABOUT IT.

LAST OF ALL, THEY OPENED MY KEG OF PROVISIONS. BEING RELIGIOUS ABSTAINERS FROM MEAT, THEY WERE HORROR STRUCK IN FINDING THE BEEF AND PORK. AFTER A LONG CONSULTATION THEY EXAMINED THE PIECES WITH A LONG FORK.

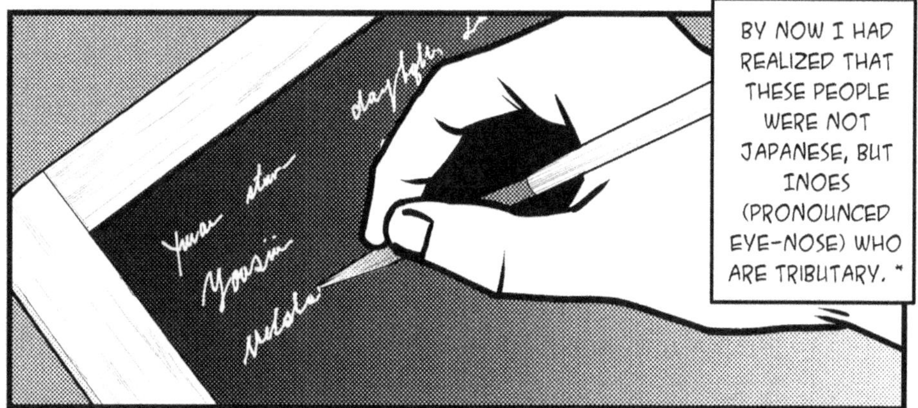

BY NOW I HAD REALIZED THAT THESE PEOPLE WERE NOT JAPANESE, BUT INOES (PRONOUNCED EYE-NOSE) WHO ARE TRIBUTARY. *

* HE MEANS AINU

I SPENT THE AFTERNOON IN WRITING INO WORDS ON MY SLATE; WHICH SEEMED TO GREATLY AMUSE THE ONLOOKERS.

THE ALTAR WAS SOMEWHAT LIKE A SMALL BOOK CASE, PLACED AGAINST THE WALL, AND DECORATED WITH VERY HIDEOUS IMAGES OF FANTASTIC SHAPE. THE CEREMONIES WERE SIMPLE:

IN THE EVENING I RECONNOITERED THE OUTBUILDINGS, AND AMONGST THEM WAS A SMALL ONE, WHICH WAS A PLACE OF WORSHIP. THE ONLY ACTS OF WORSHIP I WITNESSED WERE PERFORMED, MORNING AND EVENING, BY THE JAPANESE.

43

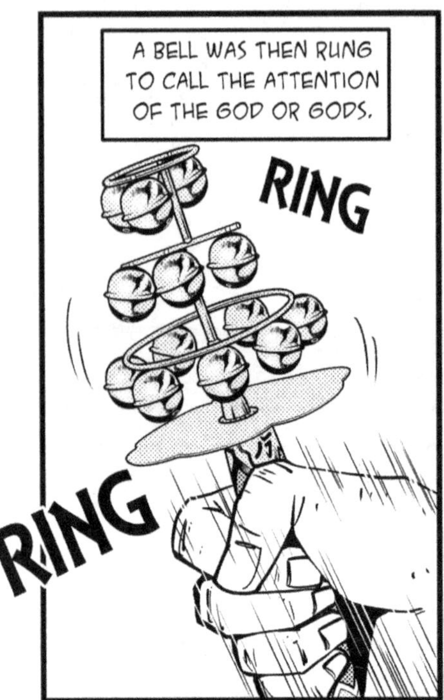

A BELL WAS THEN RUNG TO CALL THE ATTENTION OF THE GOD OR GODS.
RING
RING

BEFORE SAYING PRAYERS, SAKE WAS PLACED ON THE ALTAR.

I NEVER SAW THE INOES WORSHIP AT ANY ALTAR; BUT BEFORE MEALS THEY POUR LIQUOR INTO A BOWL, AND SPRINKLE IT IN FOUR DIRECTIONS: TOWARDS HEAVEN, AS AN OFFERING TO THE SUN··· THEN TO THE RIGHT, TO THE GOD OF THE SEA··· THEN TO THE LEFT, TO THE GOD OF THE EARTH··· AND FORWARDS, TO THE GOD OF FIRE.

THE WORSHIPPERS, KNEELING, ASSUMED THE ATTITUDE AND LOOK OF DEVOTION. THEY APPEARED TO BE VERY PARTICULAR AS TO THE MANNER OF HOLDING THEIR HANDS IN THE ACT OF PRAYER.

ON THE THIRD DAY, KECHINZA RETURNED, AND TOLD ME THAT HE WAS GOING TO SOYA, ABOUT TWENTY MILES TO THE SOUTH, IN NORTH HOKKAIDO.
宗谷の駐屯地に行って
あなたのことを
報告します。
ABOUT ME?

THERE WAS NOT MUCH ABOUT THE POOR HUTS TO DELIGHT THE EYE.

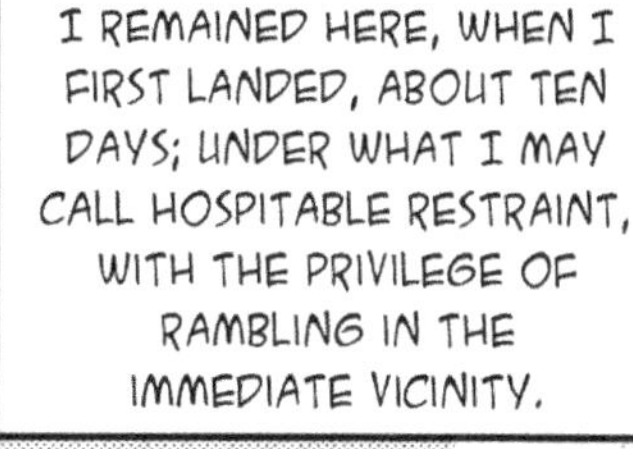

I REMAINED HERE, WHEN I FIRST LANDED, ABOUT TEN DAYS; UNDER WHAT I MAY CALL HOSPITABLE RESTRAINT, WITH THE PRIVILEGE OF RAMBLING IN THE IMMEDIATE VICINITY.

TANGARO, A VERY INTELLIGENT JAPANESE, ONE OF THE STAFF IN CHARGE, WAS MY CONSTANT COMPANION.

POINTING TO OBJECTS, WITH EYE AND MOUTH AND EAR OPEN, HE WOULD ASK THE NAMES IN ENGLISH, WHICH SEEMED TO DEEPLY IMPRESS UPON HIS MEMORY.
THIS WHAT?
THAT'S A TREE.
TREEE…
わかりました

HIS DESIRE TO LEARN ENGLISH SEEMED TO BE INTENSE.

NO, NO,
THE SOUND IS 'BOOO-K'.

WE CALL THAT A 'BOOK'.
BOHK

"本"です
HOHN?
YES, YES!

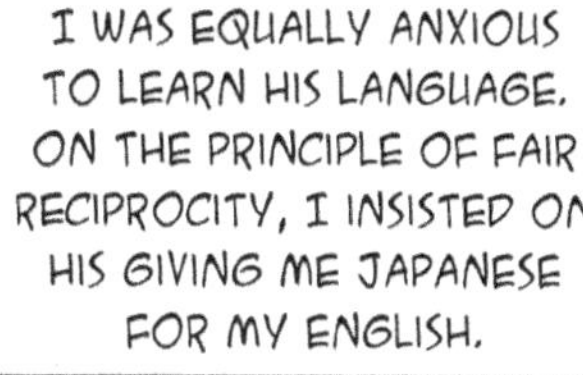
I WAS EQUALLY ANXIOUS TO LEARN HIS LANGUAGE. ON THE PRINCIPLE OF FAIR RECIPROCITY, I INSISTED ON HIS GIVING ME JAPANESE FOR MY ENGLISH.

SO, WHAT IS IT IN JAPANESE?

HOHN!
BOO-K!

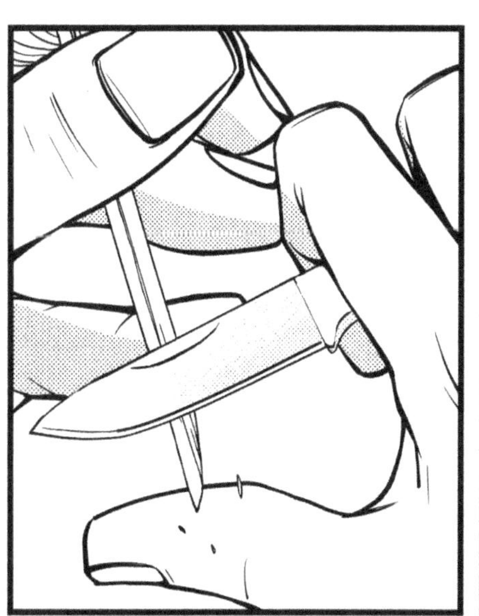

TO THE SURPRISED INTEREST OF ALL, I MADE A PEN OUT OF A CROW QUILL, TO AID ME IN THE RECORDING OF THE PHONOGRAPHIC VOCABULARY OF WORDS.

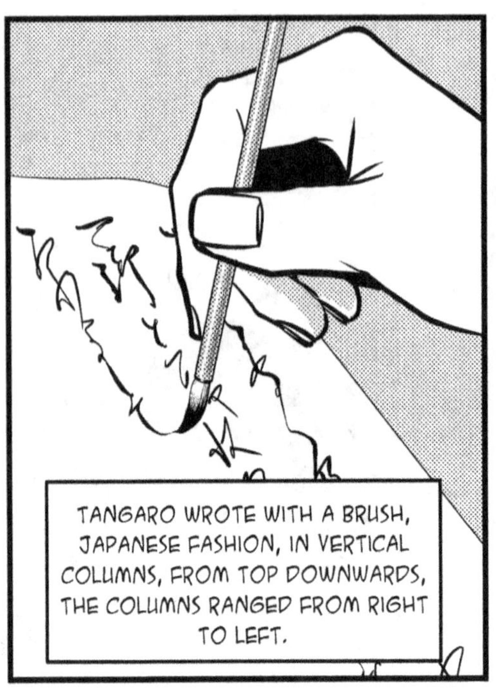

TANGARO WROTE WITH A BRUSH, JAPANESE FASHION, IN VERTICAL COLUMNS, FROM TOP DOWNWARDS, THE COLUMNS RANGED FROM RIGHT TO LEFT.

I SOON UNDERSTAND THAT IT WAS CONTRARY TO RULE AND DESIRE FOR ME TO MAKE MY NOTES. STILL, I MANAGED TO KEEP UP THE HABIT.

HIS CHARACTERS I TOOK FOR CHINESE, WITH OTHERS SEEMING TO BE THEIR OWN OF SIMPLER FORM. I DON'T KNOW CHINESE, BUT WHEN I SEE IT I THINK I RECOGNIZE IT.

ONE DAY TANGARO FURTIVELY LED ME INTO A FIELD OF LONG COARSE STANDING GRASS NEAR THE SEA SHORE, SOME DISTANCE FROM THE VILLAGE.

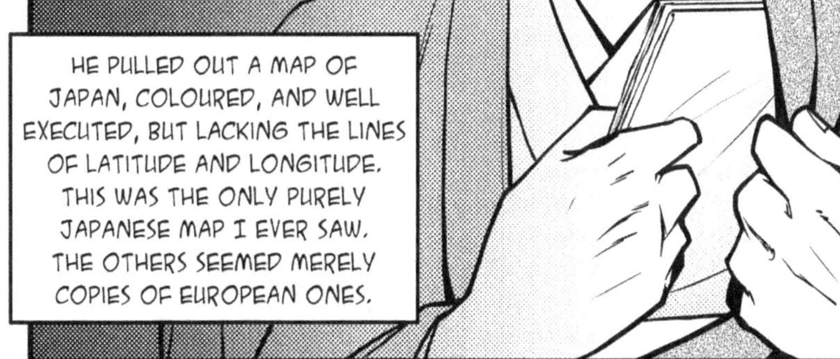
HE PULLED OUT A MAP OF JAPAN, COLOURED, AND WELL EXECUTED, BUT LACKING THE LINES OF LATITUDE AND LONGITUDE. THIS WAS THE ONLY PURELY JAPANESE MAP I EVER SAW. THE OTHERS SEEMED MERELY COPIES OF EUROPEAN ONES.

WHY IT WAS NECESSARY TO BE SO SECRETIVE I WILL EXPLAIN LATER. HE ASKED ME TO POINT OUT WHERE THE PLYMOUTH WAS WHEN I LEFT HER. HE ALSO ASKED WHETHER I HAD BEEN AT THE SOUTHERN PORTS OF JAPAN.

WE WERE NOW IN THE EXTREME NORTH OF JAPAN IN THE HOMELAND OF THE INOES. LET ME SAY A BIT MORE ABOUT THEM NOW. THEY WERE TRIBUTARY TO JAPAN, BUT A DISTINCTIVE PEOPLE IN PHYSIQUE AND MENTAL CHARACTERISTICS.
TO ME THEY SEEMED A SIMPLE KINDLY PEOPLE; AND I SHALL EVER GRATEFULLY REMEMBER THEIR SAMARITAN KINDNESS TO ME.
STRONGER IN BODY ON THE WHOLE; HEAVILY BEARDED AND VERY HAIRY GENERALLY—WHICH THE JAPANESE ARE NOT.
AS TO THEIR ORIGIN, I HAVE SEEN A GREAT MANY PEOPLE IN THE COURSE OF MY TRAVELS. TO ME THE HAIDA AND BELLA COOLA COAST INDIANS OF BRITISH COLUMBIA SEEM TO HAVE A STRIKING SIMILARITY OF PHYSICAL TYPE WITH MY STURDY FRIENDS OF YESSO.

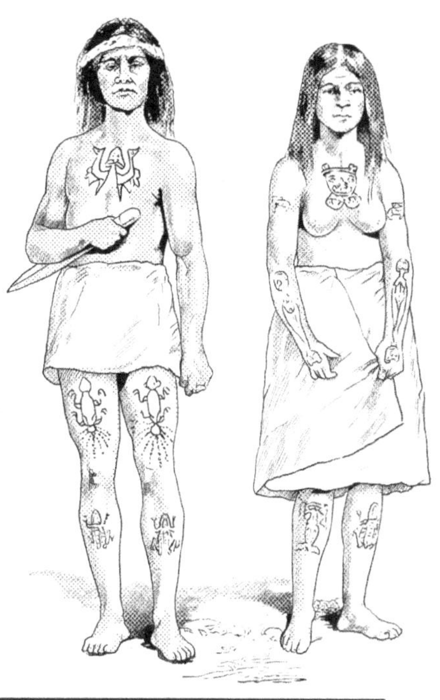

BUT IN DISPOSITION THEY DIFFER MUCH. THE NORTH WEST COAST INDIANS BEING ALL MORE OR LESS WARLIKE, AND OF AN INDEPENDENCE OF SPIRIT WHICH NEITHER FORCE NOR KINDNESS CAN SUBDUE.

NOT THAT THEY ARE UNSUSCEPTIBLE OF KINDNESS OR AMITY FROM WHITES, BUT THEY BEND TO NO MAN, AND ARE EXCEEDINGLY LORDLY, TO ALL COMERS.

INDEED, WHEN I GOT AMONGST THEM FIRST MY FEELING WAS THAT I HAD GOT INTO A NEST OF TARTARS PIRATES, WITH THEIR HEAVY BEARDS, UNCOMBED LONG HAIR, AND UNWASHED FACES.

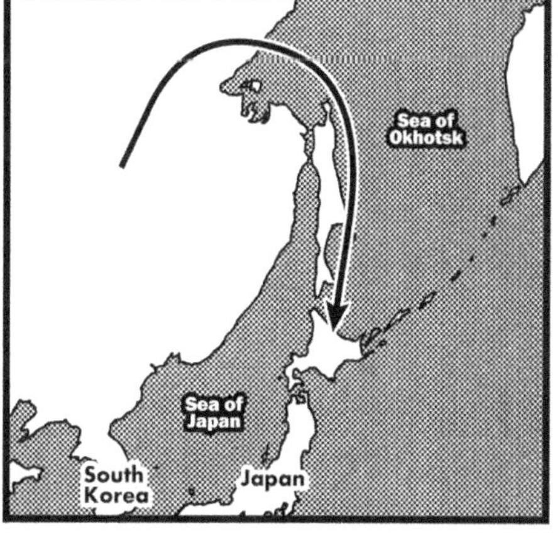

AS TO THE ORIGIN OF THESE INOES, MY IDEA IS THAT THEY CAME FROM THE MAINLAND OF ASIA, BY WAY OF THE PENINSULA OF SAKHALIN—THE TARTAR COUNTRY.

Sea of
Okhotsk
Sea of
Japan
South
Korea
Japan

ABOUT THE 11TH DAY OF MY SOJOURN IN THIS VILLAGE HALF A DOZEN OFFICERS ARRIVED IN JUNKS, AND VISITED ME.

なんと言っておる？
恐れながら、「マク－ド－ナル－ド」かと…。

TO THEIR QUESTIONS AS TO MY NAME, AND THE WHEREABOUTS OF MY SHIP, ETC., I ANSWERED, AS I HAD DONE BEFORE TO TANGARO.
名はなんと申す？
MY NAME?
I AM RANALD MACDONALD, SIR.

MY STORES WERE AGAIN MINUTELY EXAMINED, AND INVENTORIED, AND A SKETCH MADE OF EVERY ARTICLE OF INTEREST, SUCH AS MY QUADRANT BOAT, KEGS, AND ANCHOR. THEY MEASURED EVERYTHING.

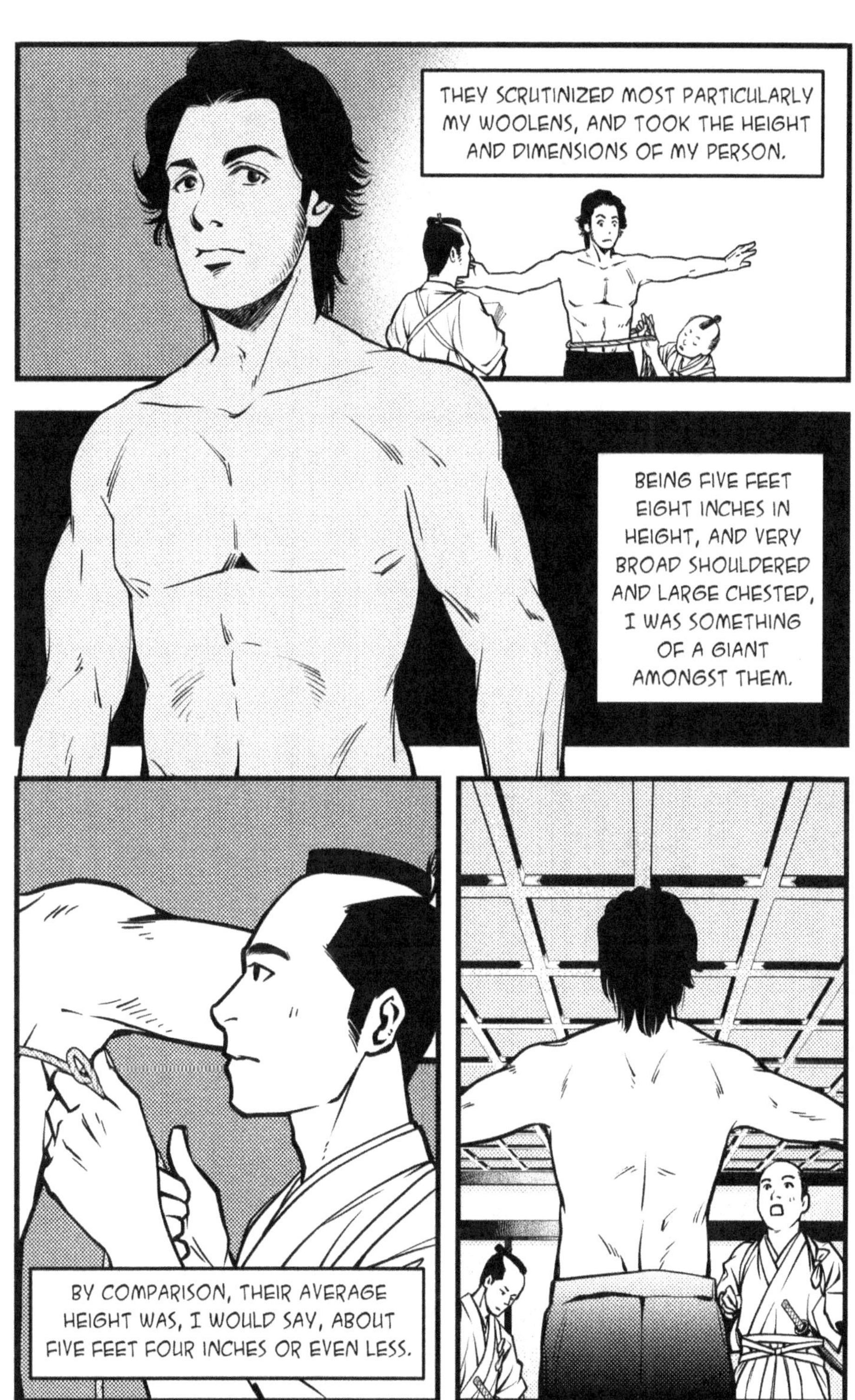

THEY SCRUTINIZED MOST PARTICULARLY MY WOOLENS, AND TOOK THE HEIGHT AND DIMENSIONS OF MY PERSON.
BEING FIVE FEET EIGHT INCHES IN HEIGHT, AND VERY BROAD SHOULDERED AND LARGE CHESTED, I WAS SOMETHING OF A GIANT AMONGST THEM.
BY COMPARISON, THEIR AVERAGE HEIGHT WAS, I WOULD SAY, ABOUT FIVE FEET FOUR INCHES OR EVEN LESS.

*NOW CALLED HONTOMARI

54

NEAR TOOTOOMARI WE WERE MET BY A BAND OF INOES. THEY ALL WENT BAREHEADED EXCEPT THE TWO OFFICERS.

WHY THESE CURTAINS WERE USED I NEVER FOUND OUT. IF INTENDED FOR CONCEALMENT FROM MY VIEW THEY CERTAINLY DID NOT WORK, FOR I COULD SEE OVER THEM.

I REMAINED IN THIS PRISON ABOUT THIRTY DAYS, DURING WHICH I LEFT THE ROOM ONLY 3 TIMES, FOR A BATH IN THE HOUSE.

I WAS LED INTO THE PRINCIPAL HOUSE, AND INTO A ROOM ABOUT TWELVE FEET SQUARE. BEING WELL FED, KINDLY ATTENDED TO I HAD NO REASON TO COMPLAIN OF MY QUARTERS.

SAYONARA, MY FRIEND.
TAKE CARE PLEASE. お達者で。
HE APPEARED TO BE MUCH AFFECTED.

IT WAS A BEAUTIFUL DAY IN EARLY AUGUST THAT I LEFT TOOTOOMARI. ON LEAVING THE HOUSE, I EXCHANGED WORDS WITH KEMON.

YOS IN YO!

OUR CONVERSATION DID NOT LAST LONG, FOR THE OFFICERS WERE TO BE ANXIOUS TO SEE ME ON BOARD THE JUNK AND BE ON OUR WAY SOUTH.

A-ME-RI-KAN SHIP?
NO, NO!
WE SAW BUT FEW BOATS. WHEN ANY WERE SEEN, THE OFFICERS WOULD DIRECT MY ATTENTION TOWARDS THEM IN CASE THEY WERE FOREIGN SHIPS, BUT ON LOOKING I COULD EASILY SEE THEY WERE NOT.

SICK?
NO, I AM QUITE WELL, THANK YOU.

WE WHEN ENTERED THE BAY OF SOYA VARIOUS BOATS CAME OUT TO MEET US.

ONCE AGAIN MY WAY WAS CURTAINED OFF. I WAS TAKEN TO GOVERNMENT HOUSE WHERE EVERYONE BOWED DEEPLY BEFORE THE SAMURAI OFFICIALS.

MY GESTURE WAS TAKEN BADLY AND I WAS TOLD TO TAKE OFF MY HAT.
脱いでください
CERTAINLY.

I WOULD NOT BE HAPPY IN A PRISON. IT CERTAINLY WOULD NOT MAKE FOR A GOOD CONNECTION BETWEEN US.
良くない。
YES,
承知仕った。

IN THE HOUSE, I WAS CONDUCTED TO A NEWLY BUILT PRISON; IT WAS SLIGHTLY PUT TOGETHER, AS IF BUILT IN A HURRY.
ACCORDING TO APPEARANCES, I THOUGHT IT WAS NOT THEIR INTENTION TO KEEP ME THERE LONG.

THEY INFORMED ME, THAT THEY WOULD, ON THE MORROW, HAVE THE WINDOWS OPEN DURING THE EVENING. AND THAT I COULD WALK TO A CONNECTED ROOM, SO I COULD RANGE ABOUT TWENTY FEET.
COULD I HAVE MORE AIR?

AGAIN, EVERYTHING OF MINE WAS CLOSELY INSPECTED. AFTERWARDS I WAS TOLD THAT THERE WERE FIVE CANNON IN SOYA, AND ABOUT A HUNDRED OFFICERS AND SOLDIERS, BUT THAT IN CASE OF NEED THEY COULD BE REINFORCED FROM OTHER STATIONS.

AND THAT NEXT DAY I WAS INTERVIEWED BY SADDO, THE COMMANDANT, A PERSON OF SEVENTY-FOUR YEARS OF AGE, BUT LOOKED YOUNGER.

*THE USA AND FRANCE ARE PHYSICALLY LARGER THAN JAPAN, BUT THE UK IS SLIGHTLY SMALLER, EVEN WITH THE WHOLE OF IRELAND INCLUDED IN THE UK, AS IT WAS IN 1848.

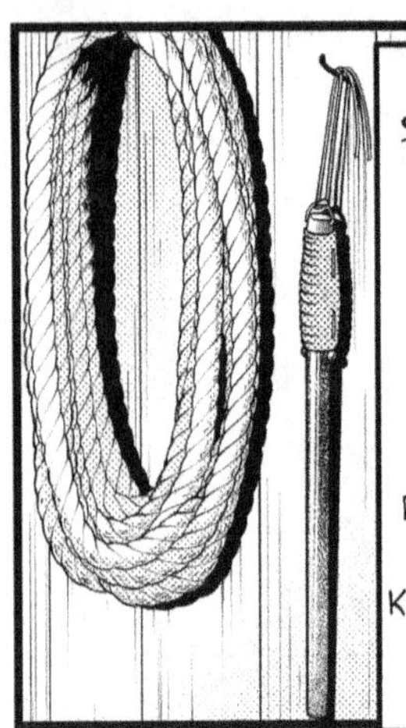

*THE CORRECT SPELLING IS MATSUMAE.

*HIS NAME WAS ACTUALLY OBA, STATIONED AT SOYA.

60

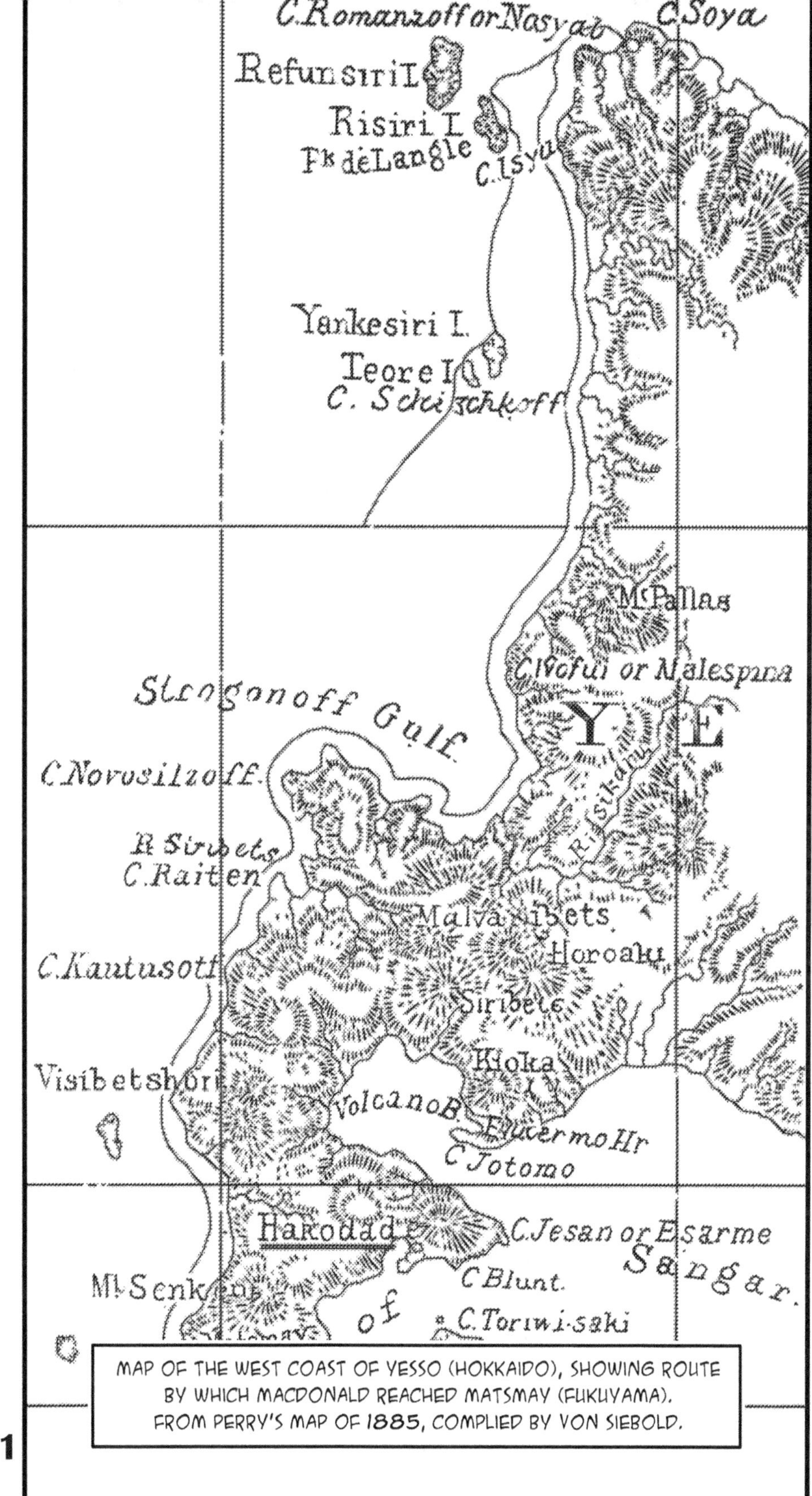

MAP OF THE WEST COAST OF YESSO (HOKKAIDO), SHOWING ROUTE
BY WHICH MACDONALD REACHED MATSMAY (FUKUYAMA).
FROM PERRY'S MAP OF 1885, COMPILED BY VON SIEBOLD.

IN THE BEGINNING OF SEPTEMBER, ABOUT 15 DAYS LATER, WE ARRIVED AT THE WONDERFUL BAY AT MATSMAI. WE PASSED NUMBER OF SMALL ISLANDS ON THE SOUTHERN PART OF THE ISLAND OF MATSMAI.

A MEMBER WENT ASHORE TO REPORT OUR ARRIVAL TO THE CHIEF THERE. AND NOT LONG AFTER MANY BOATS ARRIVED FULL OF JAPANESE OFFICERS, SOME OF HIGH RANK.

30 OR MORE CROWDED IN TO SEE ME. I WAS LOOKED AT AS IF AN ANIMAL ON DISPLAY, WHICH ANNOYED ME. I FELT, HOWEVER, I HAD TO DO SOMETHING.

"THE CHIEF SAMURAI OF THE AREA WAS SURPRISED BY HOW MUCH MACDONALD RESEMBLED A JAPANESE PERSON.
NAGASAKI, GO AWAY.
日本人ではないか！ *
I TOOK THIS TO MEAN THEY WOULD MAKE OR REPAIR A SHIP TO TAKE ME TO NAGASAKI, ABOUT 1,000 MILE SOUTH.
CARPENTER. SHIP!
NAGASAKI, YOU GO.
NO! NO! YOU NAGASAKI GO AWAY!
WHY TAKE ALL THAT TROUBLE?
WHY NOT ALLOW ME TO REMAIN AMONG YOU?

SO, LATER I WAS TAKEN ASHORE. THE WHOLE NEIGHBORHOOD WAS CROWDED WITH PEOPLE TRYING TO CATCH A GLIMPSE OF ME.
THEY ALL GAZED AT ME AS IF I WERE A WILD BEAST. I COULD NOT STAND IT, SO I HID IN THE PALANQUIN AS MUCH AS POSSIBLE.
ON THE WALL, I SAW TWO ENGLISH LETTERS, J AND C, WRITTEN WITH CHARCOAL. SEEING THIS, A LONG TRAIN OF CONJECTURES FLASHED THROUGH MY BRAIN.
THE GOVERNOR OF THE AREA GREETED ME IN A FRIENDLY MANNER, AND LED ME TO A PLEASANT ROOM THAT WAS A CHEERFUL WELCOME.

SEEING MY CURIOSITY THEY SHOWED ME THE RIDGE POLE OF THE ROOF ON WHICH WERE WRITTEN VARIOUS NAMES: I COULD MAKE OUT ROBERT MCCOY, JOHN BRADY, AND ANOTHER, JOHN SOMETHING – THE REST OF THIS NAME AND THE OTHER NAMES I COULD NOT MAKE OUT.

A-MERI-KA!
Robert McCoy
John Brady
John m...
OH, THEY CAME FROM AMERICA?

BY GESTURES AND OUR HALF COMMUNICATION THEY MADE ME UNDERSTAND THAT FIFTEEN AMERICANS HAD MADE THEIR ESCAPE FROM HERE, HAD BEEN CAUGHT, HAND-CUFFED, DRAGGED BACK, AND "HAD THEIR THROATS CUT"

I AFTERWARDS LEARNED THAT THIS WAS THE SAME AMERICAN CREW THAT WAS DELIVERED UP AT NAGASAKI WHEN I WAS. THEIR STORY, WHICH I LEARNED AFTER LEAVING JAPAN, IS AS FOLLOWS:

AND POINTING TO AN IRON BLUDGEON HANGING IN THE GUARD ROOM; MENTIONED MCCOY'S NAME AND MADE ME UNDERSTAND THAT HE HAD BEEN HIT WITH IT.

THEY WERE THE CREW OF THE WHALER "LAGODA," WHO HAD DESERTED HER NEAR MATSMAI. THERE WERE FIFTEEN OF THEM, EIGHT FROM THE UNITED STATES AND SEVEN SANDWICH ISLANDERS. THEY WERE TREATED KINDLY BUT BEING YOUNG AND VIOLENT, QUARRELED AMONGST THEMSELVES AND GAVE MUCH TROUBLE.

MCCOY HIMSELF MADE 2 OR EVEN 3 ATTEMPTS TO ESCAPE, ONE WITH THE AMERICAN JOHN BULL.

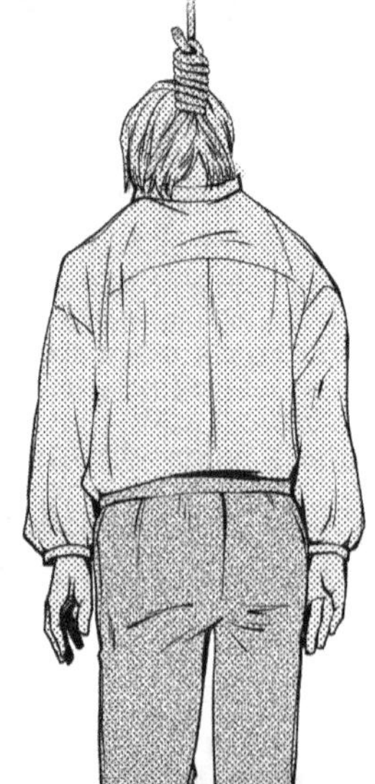

DESPITE GOOD CARE, ONE AMERICAN DIED A NATURAL DEATH, AND ONE SANDWICH ISLANDER HUNG HIMSELF'.

AS TO MYSELF, ONE DAY THE GOVERNOR GAVE ME A PRESENT OF JAPANESE CLOTHING, TWO KNIVES, A BOX OF CONFECTIONERY,
WITH A PRESENTATION CARD CONSISTING OF A PIECE ABOUT THE SIZE OF HALF A SHEET OF NOTE PAPER, FOLDED UP IN A PECULIAR FORM, THE ENDS TIED WITH BOWS OF PAPER—PAPER VERY THIN, FINE AND GLOSSY.

I WAS ALSO PRESENTED WITH A BED AND COVERING, A LARGE GOWN THICKLY PADDED, AND A PILLOW OF VARNISHED WOOD, A SMALL PILLOW. I ASKED FOR MY CHEST, TO GET AT MY BOOKS. IT WAS REFUSED AT FIRST.

HOLY BIBLE
THEY UNDERSTOOD AND GAVE ME MY BIBLE. AT MY REQUEST, THEY EVEN MADE A SHELF FOR IT. THEY SEEMED TO RESPECT THE BIBLE, RECOGNIZING IT AS SOME KIND OF HOLY BOOK.

GOD! KAMI!
聖なる本を ご所望か？

WE EMBARKED IN AN OPEN BOAT, SOMEWHAT SIMILAR TO THE ONE IN TOOTOOMARI, BUT THERE WERE NO OARS OTHER THAN THAT OF THE STEERSMAN. WE MADE FOR A LARGE JUNK, THE "TENJINMARU", ABOUT THREE MILES OFF.

I REMAINED THERE ABOUT TWENTY DAYS UNTIL THE OFFICIAL ORDER FOR MY DEPARTURE WAS FORMALLY RECEIVED, AT THE BEGINNING OF OCTOBER. AGAIN, THEY SHOOK HANDS WITH ME AT PARTING, AND EXPRESSED REGRET.

THE MAIN CABIN WAS NEAR MY 'CAGE'. I NOTICED THAT BEFORE EATING, THE JAPANESE PUT THE CHOP STICKS TO THE FOREHEAD, AS IF SAYING GRACE.

I WAS PUT INTO A SMALL GRATED CABIN. LIKE A CAGE. THERE I REMAINED ALL THE REST OF THE VOYAGE, UNABLE TO SEE ANYTHING OUTSIDE EXCEPT ON TWO OR THREE OCCASIONS. I COMPLAINED ABOUT SUCH CLOSE CONFINEMENT, SO THE CAPTAIN ORDERED THE GRATES REMOVED.

THE LEAVES WERE THIN, DOUBLED, AND PRINTED ONLY ON ONE SIDE. THE PAPER IS MUCH THINNER AND MORE TRANSPARENT THAN ANY

IN THE BOOKS THE "FOOT NOTES" ARE AT THE TOP OF THE PAGE; AND THE TITLE PAGE IS AT WHAT WE

* RM MEANS ERAMACHI IN HOKKAIDO.

*ACTUALLY TATSUNOSHIN SHIRAI.

*1 ACTUALLY TATSUNOSHIN SHIRAI.

*2 ACTUALLY SAKUSHICHIRO UEMURA AND EINOSUKE MORIYAMNA, WHO WOULD BECOME AN IMPORTANT FIGURE IN LATER NEGOTIATIONS WITH WESTERN GOVERNMENTS.

*HIS NAME WAS ACTUALLY JOSEPH HENRY LEVYSSOHN, THE HEAD OF THE DUTCH FACTORY IN DEJIMA FROM 1845 TO 1850. IN THIS CASE 'FACTOR' MEANS SOMETHING LIKE AGENT.

NAGASAKI IS A CITY OF, I SHOULD SAY, ABOUT TEN THOUSAND HOUSES. THE HOUSES, THOUGH SMALL COMPARED TO OURS OF OUR CITIES, SEEMED, ON THE WHOLE, TO BE OF A BETTER CLASS THAN ANY I HAD SEEN ELSEWHERE IN THE COUNTRY.

THE STREETS WERE ABOUT FIFTY TO SIXTY FEET IN WIDTH, AND WERE PAVED, IN THE MIDDLE, WITH STONE.

THE INNER HARBOR IS ABOUT FOUR MILES IN LENGTH AND ABOUT A MILE AND A HALF IN AVERAGE WIDTH. THERE WAS A DUTCH SHIP ANCHORED ABOUT TWO HUNDRED FATHOMS FROM THE SMALL ISLAND, DESSIMA, WITH ITS DUTCH FACTORY. THERE WERE ALSO THREE LARGE CHINESE JUNKS, ARMED WITH CANNON, AND MANY JAPANESE JUNKS TOO.

73

THE GATEWAY, WHICH WAS SIMILAR TO THOSE I SAW AT TOOTOOMARI AND SOYA, WAS ABOUT FIFTEEN FEET IN WIDTH AND ABOUT THIRTY FEET IN HEIGHT.
FROM IT, ALONG THE STREET, SOLDIERS, WITH SIDE ARMS, WERE STANDING IN A ROW ON EACH SIDE.

ON A SLIDING FRAME. THE HOUSES WERE NEITHER PAINTED NOR WHITEWASHED.
WE PASSED THROUGH SEVERAL STREETS OF SMALL WOODEN HOUSES, WITH PEAKED AND PROJECTING ROOFS, WINDOWS OF OILED PAPER,

THERE WERE SOME LARGER AND OF A BETTER CLASS HOUSES OF BRICK OR STONE, TWO STORIES IN HEIGHT. THESE HAD GARDENS IN FRONT, SHELTERED BY A STONE WALL, SURMOUNTED WITH BROKEN GLASS.

WE ARRIVED AT THE FOOT OF A HILL, AND THEN ASCENDED BY LARGE STONE STEPS TO THE GOVERNOR'S RESIDENCE, THREE OR FOUR HUNDRED YARDS OFF. THERE WERE THOUSANDS OF SPECTATORS.

INSIDE, I WAS MET AGAIN BY A DUTCH SPEAKING JAPANESE INTERPRETER TO SIT DOWN. THEY BROUGHT IN AND SPREAD OUT SOME DISHES FOR ME. NOT FROM HUNGER, BUT TO SHOW THAT I WAS NOT AFRAID, I ATE.

LATER, MURAYAMA CAME IN AND TOLD ME I WOULD SOON APPEAR BEFORE THE GOVERNOR.

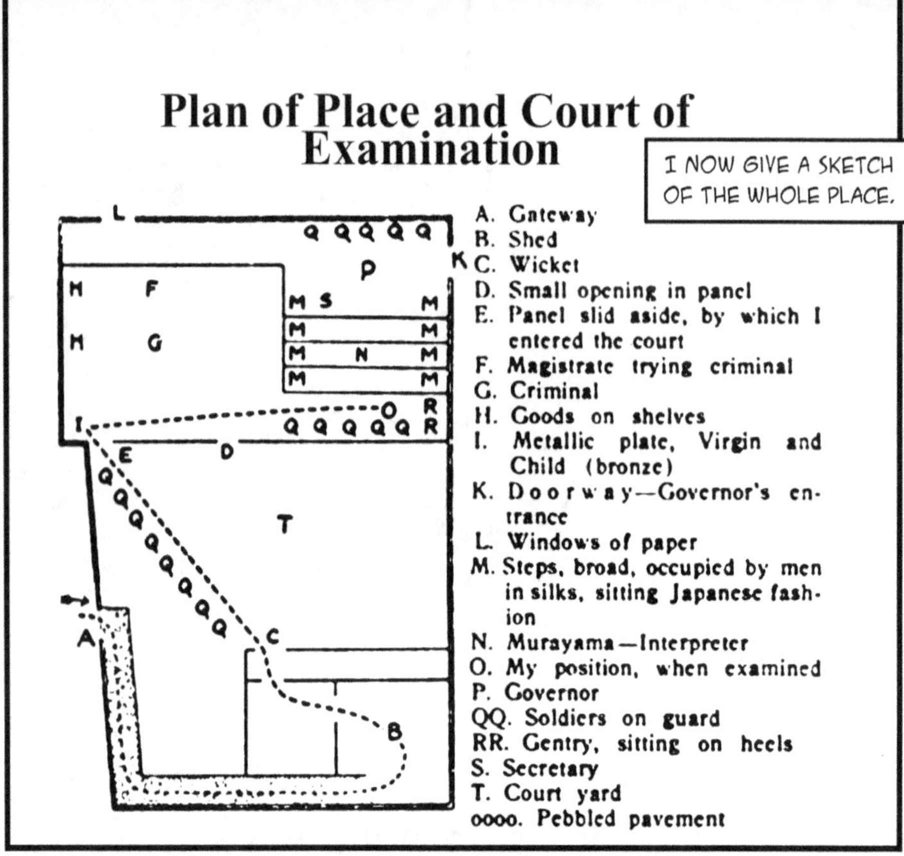

Plan of Place and Court of Examination

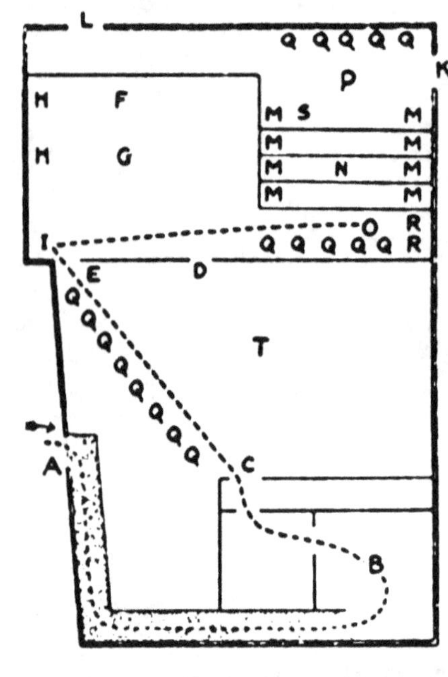

A. Gateway
B. Shed
C. Wicket
D. Small opening in panel
E. Panel slid aside, by which I entered the court
F. Magistrate trying criminal
G. Criminal
H. Goods on shelves
I. Metallic plate, Virgin and Child (bronze)
K. Doorway—Governor's entrance
L. Windows of paper
M. Steps, broad, occupied by men in silks, sitting Japanese fashion
N. Murayama—Interpreter
O. My position, when examined
P. Governor
QQ. Soldiers on guard
RR. Gentry, sitting on heels
S. Secretary
T. Court yard
oooo. Pebbled pavement

* THIS PRACTICE WAS KNOWN AS FUMI-E 踏み絵, DURING THE ANTI-CHRISTIAN CAMPAIGNS IN JAPAN.

MURAYAMA REPEATED HIS INJUNCTION TO BOW LOW. BUT, STILL FEELING PUT OUT BY SUCH TREATMENT, I DIDN'T.

CURIOUS TO READ MY FATE AT THE HANDS OF HIS EXCELLENCY, I LOOKED HIM FEARLESSLY BUT RESPECTFULLY, FULL IN THE FACE. SO DID HE ME. ALL AROUND US THEY REMAINED IN THEIR LOWLY POSITION FOR QUITE A TIME, SAY TEN OR FIFTEEN SECONDS DURING WHICH, IN DEAD SILENCE, THE GOVERNOR AND I STARED AT EACH OTHER.

HAD I KNOWN THAT, I CERTAINLY WOULD HAVE ACKNOWLEDGED THE COMPLIMENT WITH A SPECIAL BOW, IN TRUE FREEMAN'S STYLE, WITH A WAVE OF THE HANDS.

YET AGAIN THEY ASKED ME MANY QUESTIONS. MURAYAMA, INTERPRETED TO THE GOVERNOR, ADDRESSING HIM IN A FULL DISTINCT TONE, RESPECTFULLY—BOWING AT THE END OF EACH SENTENCE, RESTING ON HIS HANDS ON THE GROUND, HIS EYES CAST DOWN, AND AT THE CONCLUSION OF EVERY SENTENCE INHALING AUDIBLY THROUGH HIS TEETH, AS IF AFRAID OF OFFENDING.

I WAS BROUGHT UP AN EPISCOPALEAN, AS WAS MY SCOTTISH FATHER'S CREED, TO BELIEVE IN GOD AND IN JESUS CHRIST, HIS ONLY SON, BORN OF THE VIRGIN MA...
PLEASE TELL MORE.

YET AGAIN THEY ASKED ME MANY QUESTIONS.
THE GOVERNOR ASK: YOU BELIEVE IN GOD?
YES!

THAT WILL DO! THAT WILL DO!

HE THEN TRANSLATED MY ANSWER TO THE GOVERNOR, REFRAINING—I BELIEVE—FROM ANY MENTION OF THE "VIRGIN MARY," OR "CHRIST." IN THAT, HE WAS MY FRIEND, INDEED! AFTERWARDS I WAS TOLD THAT A COMFORTABLE HOUSE WOULD BE PREPARED FOR ME.

IN MY SMALL ROOM, THE JAPANESE BED AND CLOTHES, AND A LOOKING GLASS WHICH I HAD GOT FROM THE GOVERNOR OF MATSMAI WERE RETURNED TO ME. I HAD THE USE, ALSO, OF A MOSQUITO BAR CURTAIN WHICH WAS NECESSARY EVEN THEN—OCTOBER— THE WEATHER BEING FINE AND MILD.
I WILL BE LONESOME HERE WITH NO BOOKS AND LITTLE COMPANY, APART FROM YOUR GOOD SELF.
IF YOU GOOD, THE GOVERNOR WILL GIVE YOU EVERYTHING YOU WANT.
THIS SOUNDED PROMISING. BUT AT FIRST I WAS TREATED COOLLY. THERE WAS A GUARD OVER ME, NIGHT AND DAY; AND MY ROOM WAS ALWAYS LOCKED.

IF I CAN NOT GET MY OTHER BOOKS, MAY I HAVE MY BIBLE AT LEAST?
DON'T MENTION THE NAME OF BIBLE IN JAPAN, IT IS BAD BOOK.

WHEN I POINTED OUT BATTAN IN THE CHINA SEA, AS THE LAST PORT AT WHICH THE VESSEL I LEFT HAD TOUCHED THEY CONVERSED A LONG TIME ABOUT IT, USING OFTEN THE WORD "PADRE".

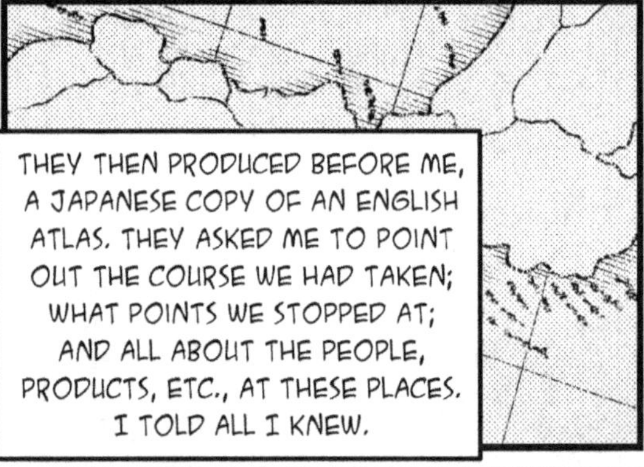

I OFTEN, AFTER THAT, SPOKE TO HIM ON THE SUBJECT. HE SAID THE CAUSE OF THE LAW WAS THE REVOLUTIONARY CONDUCT OF THE PORTUGESE CHRISTIANS EARLY IN THE SEVENTEENTH CENTURY, FOR WHICH THEY WERE EXPELLED, AND THOSE REMAINING UTTERLY ANNIHILATED IN THE LAND.

Nish Youtchero (Nishi Yoichiro),
Wirriamra Saxtuero (Uyemura Sakuschichiro),
Murayama Yeanoske (Moriyama Einosuke), Nish Kataro (Nishi Keitaro),
Akawa Keijuro (Ogawa Keijuro), Shoya Tanasabero (Shioya Tanesaburo),
Nakiama Shoma (Nakayama Hyoma), Enomade Dinoske (Inomata Dennosuke),
Sujuke Tatsuetsero (Shizuki Tatsuichiro), Hewashe Yasaro (Iwase Yashiro),
Inderego Horn (Hori Ichiro), Shegie Taganotske (Shige Takanosuke),
Namra Tsenoske (Namura Tsunenosuke),
Notoke Sayemon (Motoki Shosayemon).

THEIR HABIT WAS TO READ ENGLISH TO ME; ONE AT A TIME.
VERY GOOD, BUT THE PRONUNCIATION IS A LITTLE WRONG.
発音は 'POP-YOU-LAY-SHIN'
THE POP-UU-LAH-TEE-ON OF LONDON IS….
MY DUTY WAS TO CORRECT THEIR PRONUNCIATION, AND USING THE BASIC JAPANESE I HAD PICKED UP TO EXPLAIN MEANING, CONSTRUCTION, ETC.
IT WAS DIFFICULT TO MAKE THEM CATCH SOME OF OUR SOUNDS, ESPECIALLY THE CONSONANTS WERE DIFFICULT FOR THEM.
HA HA!
FOR INSTANCE: THEY CANNOT PRONOUNCE, EXCEPT VERY IMPERFECTLY, THE LETTER L. THEY PRONOUNCE IT R. SO THAT THEY RENDERED MY NAME RANARDO MACDONARDO, WITH A STRONG BURR OF THE R. THEY ALSO HAD A HABIT OF ADDING A SHORT I OR A OR O AT THE END OF CONSONANTS.
THERE IS NO 'A' SOUND AT THE END THERE. JUST SAY 'FOOD' NOT 'FOOD-O'.
THEY WERE ALL WELL UP IN GRAMMAR, AND THEY LEARNED IT READILY FROM ME. THEY WERE ALL VERY QUICK, AND RECEPTIVE. IT WAS A PLEASURE TO TEACH THEM.
ああ、難しいですね！
FOO-DO, FOOD-O.
?

WITHOUT BOASTING TOO MUCH I THINK I PICKED UP THEIR LANGUAGE EASILY, MANY OF THEIR WORDS SOUNDING FAMILIAR TO ME—POSSIBLY THROUGH MY MATERNAL ANCESTRY.
THIS IS 山 , IT MEAN MOUNTAIN.
わかりました

THE DISCUSSIONS ABOUT DIFFERENT APPLICATIONS OF WORDS WERE A LITTLE LABORIOUS, BUT, BY AID OF THE DICTIONARIES, GENERALLY SATISFACTORY.

AND I DISCOVERED THAT I HAD A NATURAL APTITUDE FOR SUCH TEACHING – WHICH I HAD NO IDEA ABOUT UNTIL IT DEVELOPED BY THE EFFORT.

I HAD NO GRAMMAR OR BOOK OF INSTRUCTION, WHICH HELD BACK MY PROGRESS.
STILL, I LEARNED A GOOD DEAL IN OUR NORMAL CONVERSATIONS.

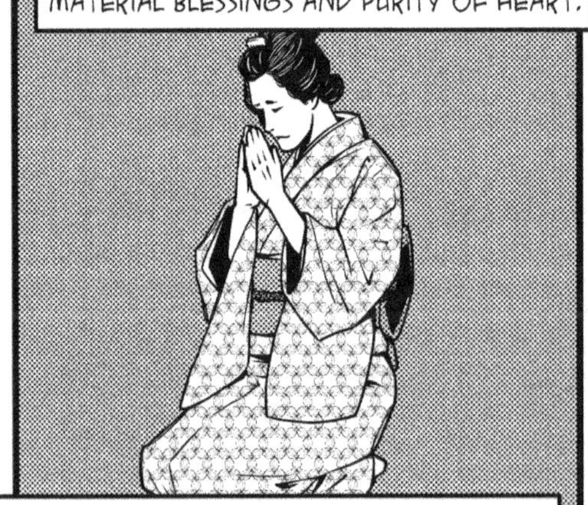

*1 AT THAT TIME, BUT THE LAW OF 1872 MADE MARRIAGE ACCEPTABLE FOR BUDDHIST MONKS.
*2 BY 'SIN' HE MEANS SHINTO.

IT WAS RARE FOR WOMEN TO VISIT ME. THE ONLY EXCEPTION WAS IN THE CASE OF ONE OF MY GUARDS, THE CAPTAIN. HE ASKED ME FOR MY CONSENT TO BRING HIS WIFE AND DAUGHTER AND THREE OTHER FEMALES.
こんにちは
MACDONARDO さん
こんにちは
CAPTAIN

THEY CAME IN, GIGGLING.
I OF COURSE, GAVE IT, FOR I WAS ANXIOUS ALSO TO SEE HOW THEIR WOMEN LOOKED.

THEIR COMPLEXION WAS A LIGHT BROWN; EYES BLACK AND SLIGHTLY OBLIQUE; NOSE SHORT, AND ALMOST STRAIGHT… FACE MORE ROUND THAN OVAL, WITH WELL-PROPORTIONED MOUTH, CHEEK BONES PROTRUSIVE… BROAD AND INTELLECTUAL FOREHEAD, FULLY EXPOSED.

I CANNOT SAY THAT THEY WERE BEAUTIFUL; NOR UGLY. THEIR GENERAL EXPRESSION OF COUNTENANCE WAS THAT OF SMILING GOOD NATURE AND ARTLESSNESS CALCULATED TO MAKE A FAVORABLE IMPRESSION.

TO JUDGE OF THEIR GENERAL DISPOSITION, I SHOULD SAY IT WAS A PREVAILING AMIABILITY.

SO FAR AS I COULD JUDGE OF THEIR FIGURES, THEY WERE SHORT AND NOT UNSHAPELY; BEARING THEMSELVES WITH A GRACEFUL MODEST DIGNITY.

THERE WAS NO TELL-TALE INTERPRETER AT THAT TIME, BUT SOME "PEEPING TOM" MUST HAVE SEEN AND TOLD THE HIGHER AUTHORITIES.

BECAUSE I DID NOT SEE THE CAPTAIN AFTER THAT, AND MISSING THIS FRIEND WHO I HAD OFTEN TALKED CLOSELY WITH, I ASKED AFTER HIM. I WAS TOLD THAT FOR BREAKING THE LAW BY BRINGING WOMEN TO MY PRISON, HIS HEAD HAD BEEN CHOPPED OFF.

I PICKED UP MORE OF THE LANGUAGE, BUT THEY REMAINED ON GUARD ABOUT SAYING TOO MUCH ABOUT THE AFFAIRS OF THE COUNTRY.
DURING THE SEVEN MONTHS AND MORE OF MY CONFINEMENT IN NAGASAKI, I DREW MORE COMFORT AND SUSTAINING COMPANIONSHIP FROM MY PUPILS, THE INTERPRETERS.

THE ONLY THING I COMPLAINED OF WAS THE SMALLNESS OF MY CAGE, BUT IN THIS I GOT NO SATISFACTION. IT WAS, THEY THOUGHT, GOOD ENOUGH FOR A SINGLE MAN. AND, AS I AFTERWARDS LEARNED, I WAS BETTER OFF THAN OTHER FOREIGN PRISONERS THEN IN CONFINEMENT.

AS THE GOVERNOR HAD PROMISED I HAD EVERYTHING I WANTED— EXCEPT LIBERTY OUTSIDE. THEY EVEN GAVE ME UP MY BIBLE; AND SEEING THAT "I MADE A GOD OF IT," THEY MADE A NEAT SHELF ("TOKIWARI") AT A CORNER OF MY ROOM, TO PUT IT ON, AS A PLACE OF HONOR.
HOLY BIBLE
HOLY BIBLE

*HARA KIRI OR SEPPUKU, AND IT DOES NOT MEAN 'HAPPY DISPATCH', THE ACTUAL MEANING OF 腹切り IS 'BELLY CUT'.

*HE MEANS BY THE SHOGUN.

90

MY SENSE OF MY SITUATION FORBADE ANY EFFORT IN THE WAY OF TEACHING A NEW FAITH TO THEM. I WENT OF THE BROAD "PLATFORM" OF A COMMON HUMANITY—THOROUGHLY IMBUED WITH THE IDEA THAT, TRULY,

SUCH BLOOD SACRIFICES ARE HARD TO BELIEVE OF SUCH A PEOPLE, SO FAR AS I COULD JUDGE FROM MY OWN OBSERVATION, PARTICULARLY THE FINE THINKING OF MY PUPILS.

THEY WERE NOT CHRISTIANS; BUT IN THEIR SENSE OF THE DEITY THEY CERTAINLY ARE NOT BELOW ANY CHRISTIAN PEOPLE THAT I EVER KNEW OR READ OF. IN MY HEART I CANNOT SAY ENOUGH ON THIS SCORE.

I BELONGED TO NO NARROW CHURCH. I WAS SIMPLY A WANDERER, FOR KNOWLEDGE—AN ADVENTURER IN THE BROAD FIELD OF ADVENTURE, FOR ADVENTURE'S SAKE.

*THERE WERE **68** PROVINCES IN THAT TIME, BEFORE THE MEIJI RESTORATION.

I BELIEVE THEY WOULD SUFFER ANNIHILATION RATHER THAN SURRENDER IN DEFENSE OF THEIR COUNTRY. UNCONQUERED; UNCONQUERABLE: THAT IS THEIR PROUD POSITION.
NATURALLY, THEY ARE BRAVE—I SHOULD SAY—UTTERLY FEARLESS OF DEATH; THEIR INSTINCTS MARKEDLY MILITARY.
UNDER THAT MASK OF PLACIDITY WHICH THEY PRESENTED, I COULD SEE THE INNER WORKING OF ASPIRATIONS FOR A HIGHER LIFE AMONGST THE NATIONS OF THE EARTH.
ACUTE ENOUGH TO PIERCE THE VEIL OF THEIR OLD TRADITIONAL LIFE, WHICH, TO THEM, WAS AS THE ROTTING SHROUD OF A DEAD PAST. THEY IMPROVED IN ENGLISH WONDERFULLY, FOR THEIR HEART WAS EVIDENTLY IN THE WORK, AND THEIR RECEPTIVENESS QUICK.
I SAW THIS MORE PARTICULARLY IN MURAYAMA AND SOME OF THE YOUNGER PUPILS WITH KEEN MINDS;

93

THE FOREIGN SHIP WHICH HAD JUST ARRIVED WAS THE AMERICAN CORVETTE, "THE PREBLE," OF EIGHTEEN GUNS, IN COMMAND OF CAPTAIN (TECHNICALLY COMMANDER) JAMES GLYNN.

INDEED?
THE CAPTAIN OF AMERICAN SHIP WANT YOUR FREEDOM.
TOMORROW YOU SEE GOVERNOR AGAIN. PAY RESPECTS.
THIS WAS NOT STRICTLY TRUE, FOR THE CAPTAIN KNEW NOTHING ABOUT ME; IT WAS THE CREW OF THE "LADOGA" THAT HE WAS AFTER.

WHILE I WAS THERE THIRTEEN AMERICAN SEAMEN WERE BROUGHT IN. THEY HAD ON THEIR ORDINARY SAILOR DRESS. I HAD ON MY JAPANESE DRESS. THEY APPEARED VERY PALE AND THIN.

THE NEW GOVERNOR HAD ARRIVED SINCE THE ARRIVAL OF THE "PREBLE," AND IN THE INTERVAL SINCE, HAD IMMEDIATELY VISITED ME, IN MY CAGE, INCOGNITO. I DID NOT KNOW THAT HE WAS THE GOVERNOR UNTIL I SAW HIM IN THE TOWN HALL, SEATED AFTERWARDS, BESIDE THE OLD GOVERNOR.

THE GOVERNOR, THROUGH INTERPRETER, THEN TOLD US OF THE ARRIVAL OF THE SHIP; AND THAT THEY HAD DECIDED ON ALLOWING US TO DEPART BY HER; BUT THAT IT WOULD BE NECESSARY FOR US TO GO TO THE DUTCH FACTORY FIRST.

THEY MADE ME KNEEL APART FROM THE REST.

CHEERY MEN, OH!
CHEERY MEN, OH!
PLEASE GIVE MY HEARTY THANKS TO BOTH THEIR EXCELLENCIES.
WHEN WE WERE IN THE DUTCH FACTORY, THE CHIEF FACTOR SAID TO US:
NO NEED TO KNEEL HERE, MEN - THIS IS A CHRISTIAN HOUSE!

96

CHEERY MEN, OH!

ON THE "PREBLE" WE WERE WARMLY WELCOMED BY HER NOBLE CAPTAIN AND RIGHT GOOD CREW.

ON BOARD THE "PREBLE," I MADE A LONG STATEMENT ABOUT MY EXPERIENCES IN JAPAN TO AN OFFICER NAMED WILSON. IT WAS TAKEN DOWN BY HIM IN WRITING AND SIGNED BY ME FOR OFFICIAL RECORD. IT IS, I UNDERSTAND TO BE FOUND IN SENATE DOCUMENTS OF 1851-1852, IX. "EXECUTIVE DOCUMENT 59," OF THE UNITED STATES.

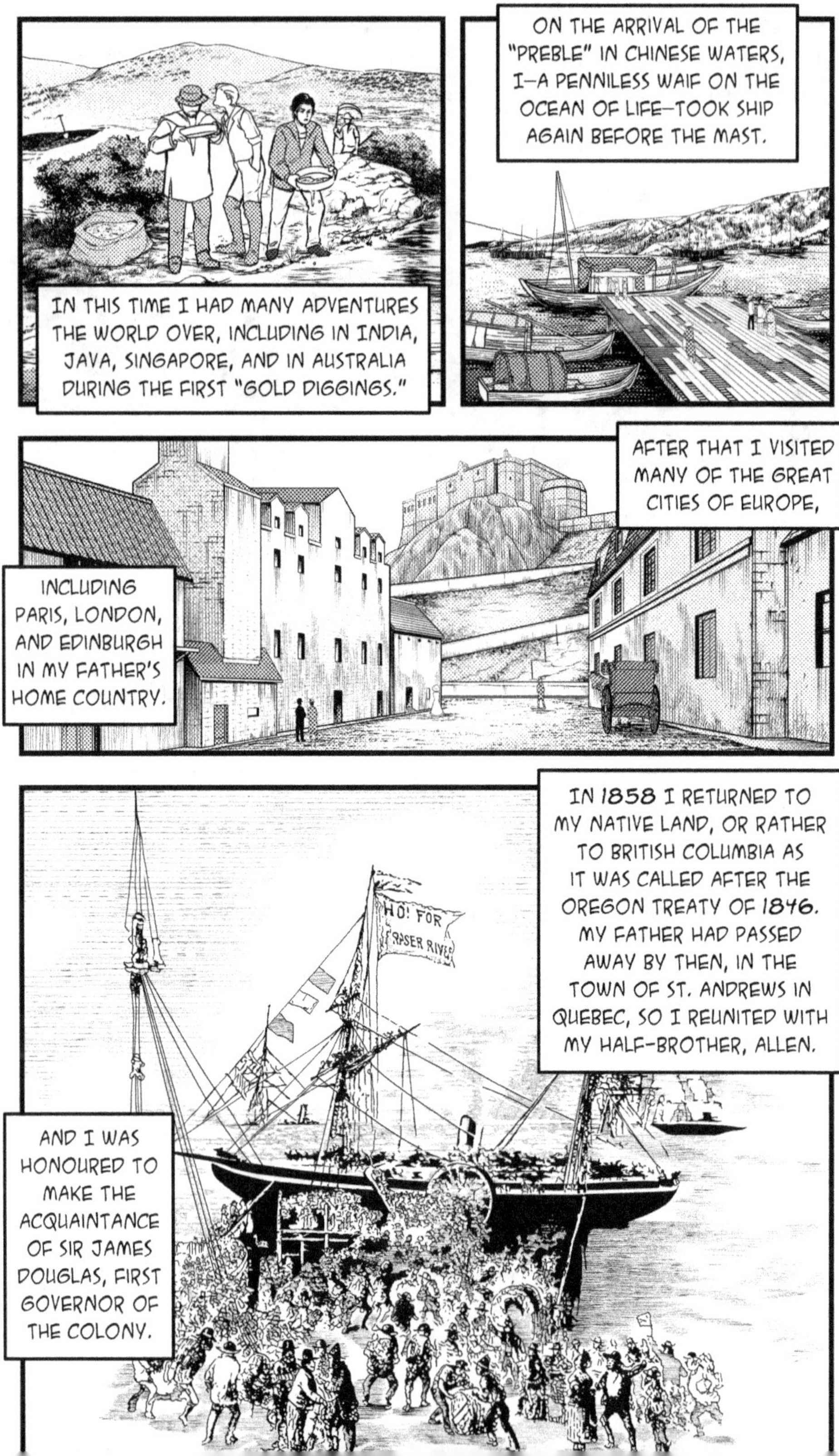

IN THIS TIME I HAD MANY ADVENTURES THE WORLD OVER, INCLUDING IN INDIA, JAVA, SINGAPORE, AND IN AUSTRALIA DURING THE FIRST "GOLD DIGGINGS."

ON THE ARRIVAL OF THE "PREBLE" IN CHINESE WATERS, I—A PENNILESS WAIF ON THE OCEAN OF LIFE—TOOK SHIP AGAIN BEFORE THE MAST.

AFTER THAT I VISITED MANY OF THE GREAT CITIES OF EUROPE,

INCLUDING PARIS, LONDON, AND EDINBURGH IN MY FATHER'S HOME COUNTRY.

IN 1858 I RETURNED TO MY NATIVE LAND, OR RATHER TO BRITISH COLUMBIA AS IT WAS CALLED AFTER THE OREGON TREATY OF 1846. MY FATHER HAD PASSED AWAY BY THEN, IN THE TOWN OF ST. ANDREWS IN QUEBEC, SO I REUNITED WITH MY HALF-BROTHER, ALLEN.

HO! FOR FRASER RIVER

AND I WAS HONOURED TO MAKE THE ACQUAINTANCE OF SIR JAMES DOUGLAS, FIRST GOVERNOR OF THE COLONY.

98

THE GOLD WORKERS WERE A ROUGH LOT AND ONE TIME I BESTED A PRIZE FIGHTER NAMED MCCUNE IN A WOODEN SINGLESTICK DUEL.

HERE I TURNED MY HAND TO SEVERAL EFFORTS OVER THE YEARS, SUCH AS WORKING AT A RANCH, AND RUNNING PACK TRAINS TO THE GOLD MINES.

I WAS OFTEN KNOWN AS 'SIWASH MACDONALD' THEN. I REMAINED AS PROUD OF MY CHINOOK ANCESTRY AS OF MY SCOTTISH.

I WOULDN'T HAVE CARED A DAMN TO BE BEATEN BY A WHITE MAN, BUT I HATE TO BE BEAT BY A SIWASH.

INDEED, AFTER THE DEATH OF KING COM-COMLY SOME OF THE OLDER PEOPLE WOULD CALL ME COMLY MACDONALD, WHICH I AM PROUD OF.

99

'EARLIER, IN 1853, AFTER RETURNING FROM EUROPE, I BECAME FRIENDS WITH MALCOLM MCLEOD, ANOTHER FINE MAN OF MIXED SCOTTISH AND NATIVE AMERICAN BLOOD. EDUCATED IN EDINBURGH, HE PRACTICED LAW IN MONTREAL. I TOLD HIM ABOUT MY STORY IN JAPAN.
WITH HIS HELP I FINISHED A FIRST DRAFT OF THIS ACCOUNT IN 1857. WE HAD GREAT TROUBLE FINDING A PUBLISHER BUT IN 1869, MY STORY WAS RELATED BY MCLEOD IN A SERIES OF ARTICLES IN THE OTTAWA TIMES, UNDER THE PEN-NAME OF BRITANNICUS.
SADLY, THE FULL BOOK WAS LONG DELAYED AND WENT THROUGH MANY DIFFICULT REVISIONS AND FALSE HOPES OF PUBLICATION, FRUSTRATINGLY DASHED.

STILL, SINCE MY TIME AMONG THE JAPANESE, I NOTE THAT THEIR RELATIONS WITH REPUBLICAN POWERS HAVE BEEN MOST AMICABLE. THE NEW PARLIAMENTARY CONSTITUTION OF JAPAN MAY BE THE DAWN—LET US HOPE—OF A BETTER DAY. FOR PEACE ON EARTH! GOOD WILL TO ALL!

Author's Note

MacDonald made various mistakes in his account, in terms of names and places. We have decided to mostly keep these to convey the experiences from his point of view and to show the confusions that cropped up.

We have also not given English translations for when the people were speaking in Japanese or Dutch. This is also to show how this confusing mix of languages was experienced by MacDonald and his Japanese hosts.

I am myself a Scottish man in Japan and have spent several holidays in the Glencoe area, where MacDonald's father was from. So it's of special interest to me to be involved in making this illustrated version of the story of a man who was probably the first ever Scot to live in Japan.

To learn more about Ranald MacDonald we recommend Frederik L. Schodt's excellent book that was very helpful during our research process: *Native American in the Land of the Shogun: Ranald Macdonald and the Opening of Japan* (Stonebridge Press). We wish to thank the Friends of MacDonald society and especially Jim Mockford for their help with this book.

**- Sean Michael Wilson,
Kumamoto, Japan**

SEAN MICHAEL WILSON is a Scottish writer living in Japan. He has written more than 40 books, published by a variety of US, UK and Japanese publishers and translated into twelve languages. In 2016 his book of Lafcadio Hearn stories, *The Faceless Ghost* was nominated for the prestigious *Eisner Book Awards*, and received a medal in the 2016 *Independent Publisher Book Awards*. His book *The Many Not the Few* has an introduction by the leader of the Labour Party and was launched at a special event in the House of Commons in 2019. In 2020 he received the Scottish Samurai Award from an association celebrating links between Japan and Scotland.

AKIKO SHIMOJIMA is a comic and manga artist from Japan. A teacher of digital comics art at a school in Tokyo, she is the illustrator of several manga and has contributed work to many other publications. Her book with Sean Michael Wilson, *Secrets of the Ninja*, got a medal in the 10th *International Manga Award*, organised by the Japanese Ministry of Foreign Affairs. Her other book with Sean Michael Wilson, The Minamata Story, received a silver medal in the 2021 *Freeman Book Awards* of Columbia University and a 2022 *Skipping Stones Award* for books about ecology.

This is the second book in Eostre's series focusing on adventure, discovery and exploration. The first was Mamiya's Maps (2022) on the explorer Mamiya Rinzō 間宮 林蔵 who mapped Sakhalin Island in the early years of the 19th century.

Mamiya's Maps is about exploration, culture clash, the making of maps and how they are related to politics. It's also anthropological in its look at the Ainu and Nivkh people of Sakhalin island. The animals and the landscape of the island and its surrounding waters are beautifully illustrated, making this a visually appealing manga that explores a little known aspect of Japanese history and culture. The issues the book covers are still relevant now, since the ownership of the island has been in dispute since the end of World War 2, but also the treatment of the Ainu and other indigenous peoples of the area has been called into question.

Reading order:

This book is read right to left, in the Japanese style. This is the last page.